EASY PIANO

TOP50s

Arranged by Dan Coates

Produced by
Alfred Music
P.O. Box 10003
Van Nuys, CA 91410-0003
alfred.com

Produced in USA.

ISBN-10: 0-7390-7788-0
ISBN-13: 978-0-7390-7788-7

Cover Photo
Moonlight Ocean: © istockphoto / ryasick

GERSHWIN®, GEORGE GERSHWIN® and IRA GERSHWIN™
Are Registered Trademarks of Gershwin Enterprises

TABLE OF CONTENTS

AS TIME GOES BY

(from *Casablanca*)

Words and Music by Herman Hupfeld
Arranged by Dan Coates

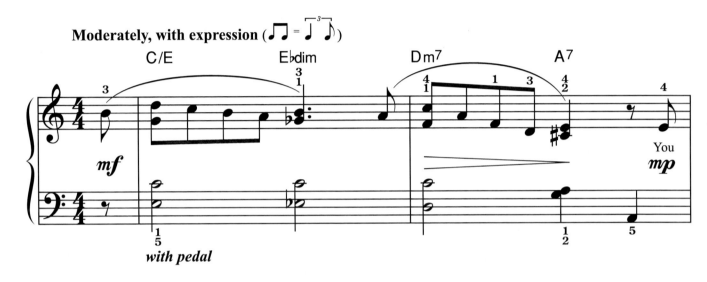

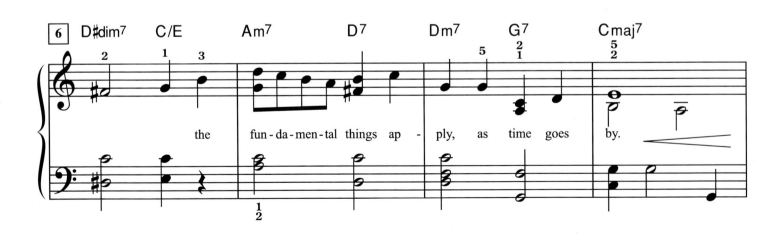

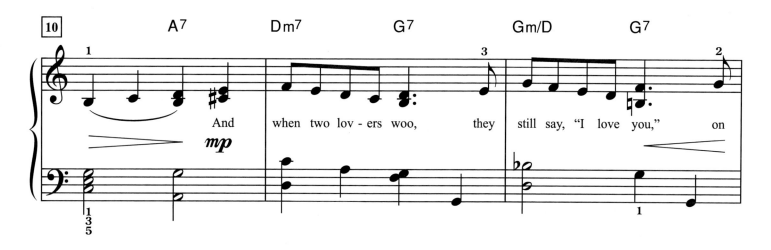

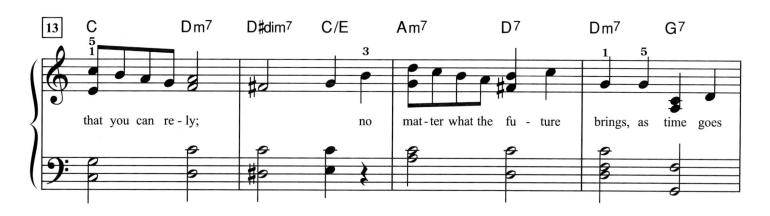

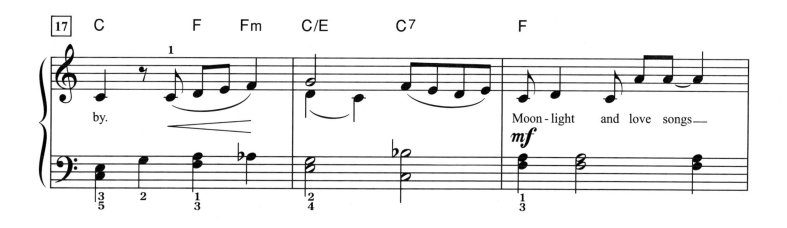

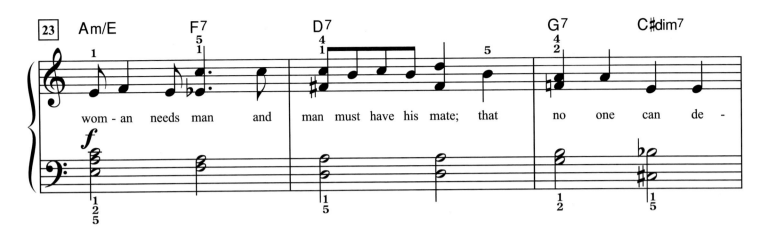

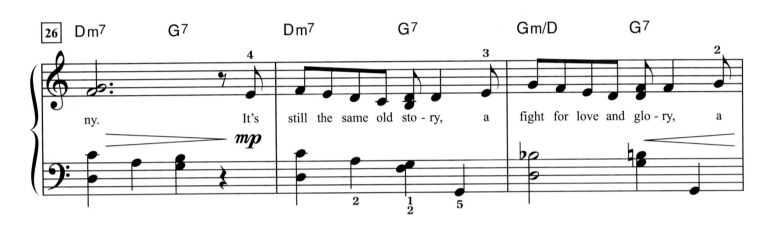

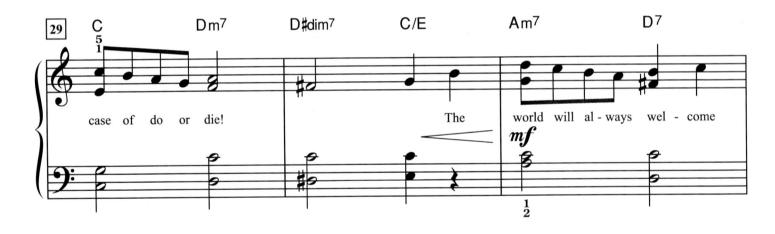

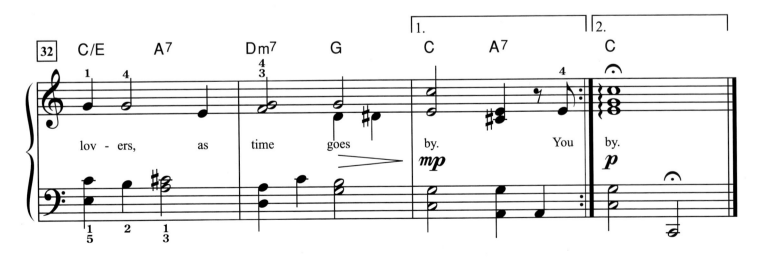

AT LAST

Music by Harry Warren
Lyrics by Mack Gordon
Arranged by Dan Coates

8

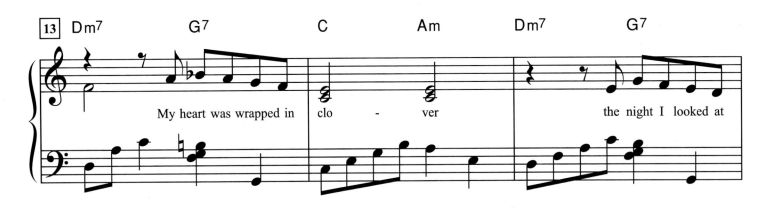

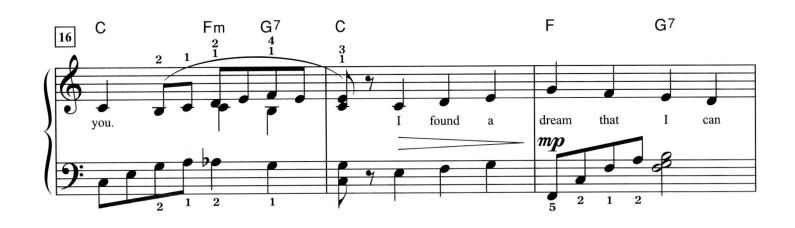

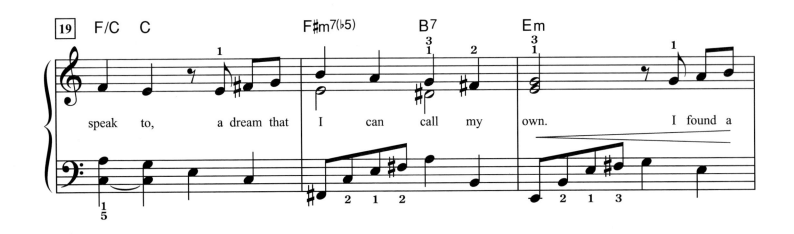

BEAUTIFUL (AS YOU)

Words and Music by
Jim Brickman, Jack Kugell and Jamie Jones
Arranged by Dan Coates

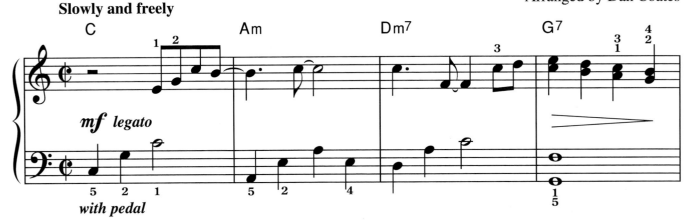

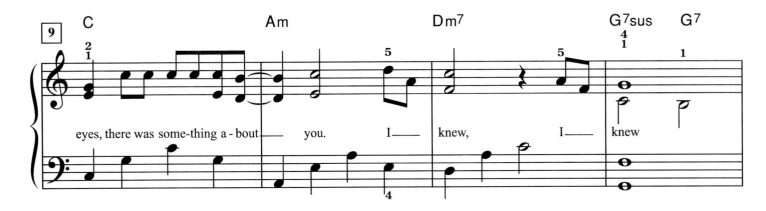

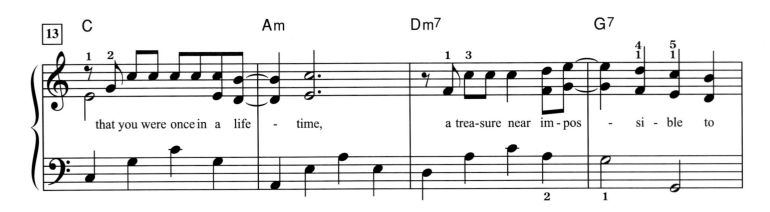

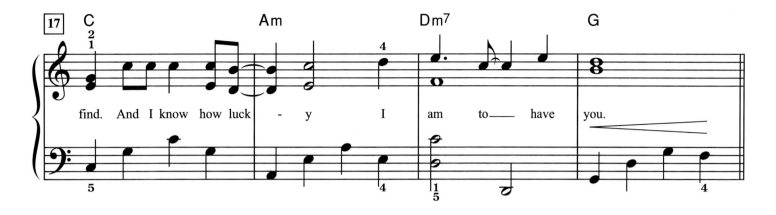

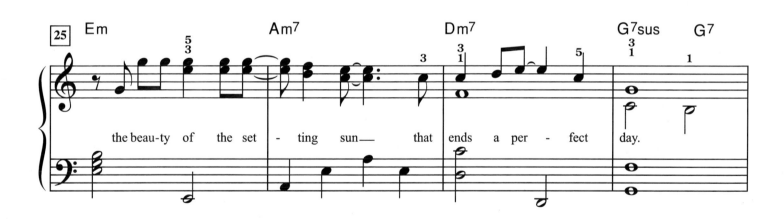

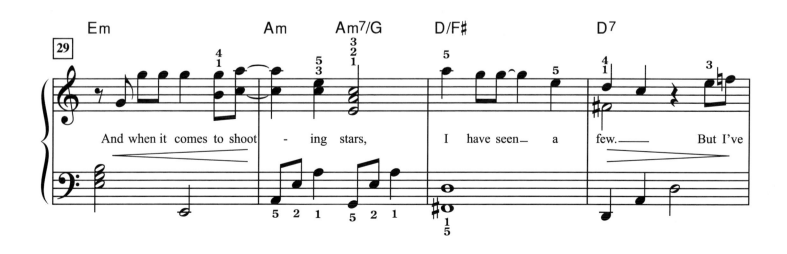

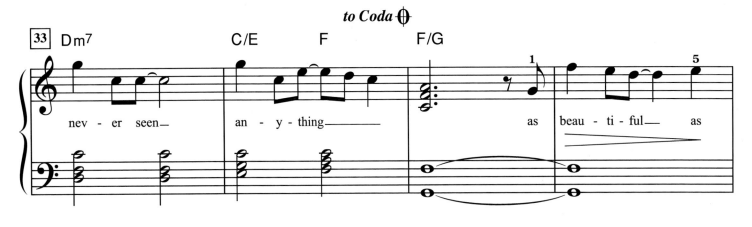

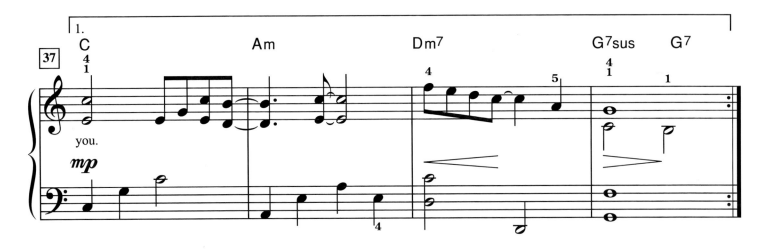

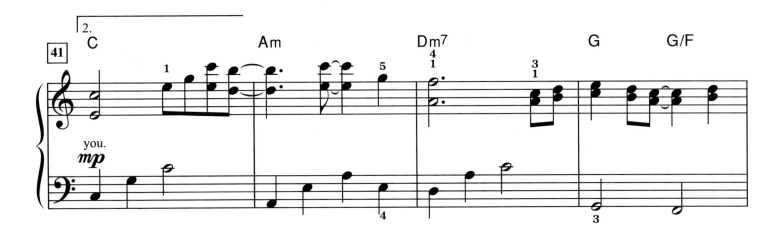

Verse 2:
Holding you in my arms,
No one else has fit so perfectly.
I could dance forever with you, with you.
And at the stroke of midnight,
Please forgive me if I can't let go,
'Cause I never dreamed I'd find
A Cinderella of my own.
(To Chorus:)

BECAUSE OF YOU

Words and Music by
Kelly Clarkson, Ben Moody and David Hodges
Arranged by Dan Coates

Verse 2:
I lose my way,
And it's not too long before you point it out.
I cannot cry,
Because I know that's weakness in your eyes.
I'm forced to fake a smile,
A laugh, every day of my life.
My heart can't possibly break
When it wasn't even whole to start with.
(To Chorus:)

BLUE MOON

Music by Richard Rodgers
Lyrics by Lorenz Hart
Arranged by Dan Coates

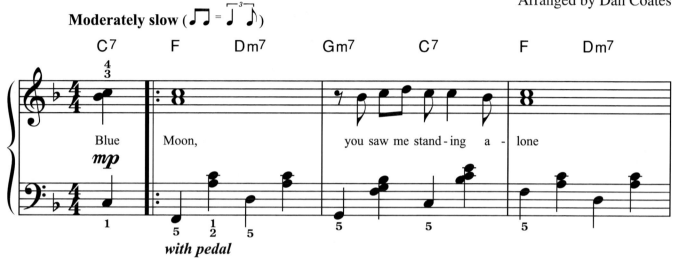

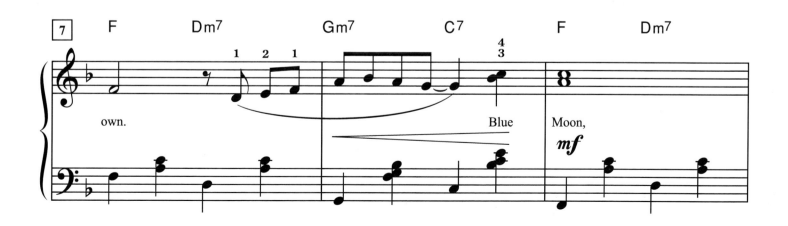

you knew just what I was there for._____ You heard me say - ing a

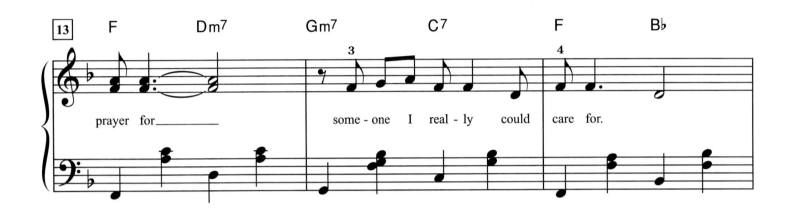

prayer for_____ some - one I real - ly could care for.

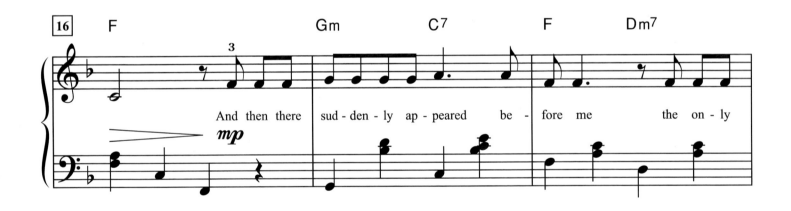

And then there sud - den - ly ap - peared be - fore me the on - ly

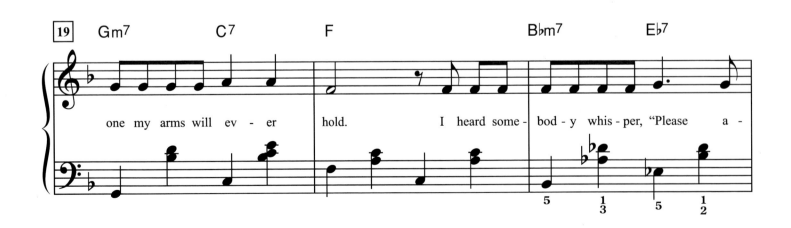

one my arms will ev - er hold. I heard some - bod - y whis - per, "Please a -

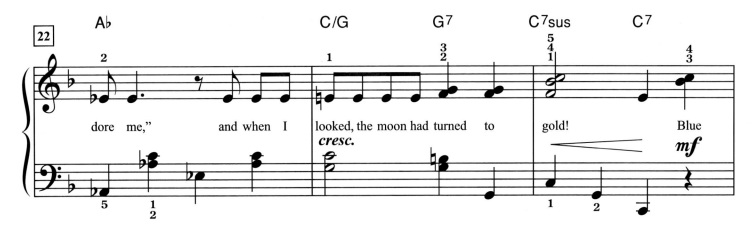

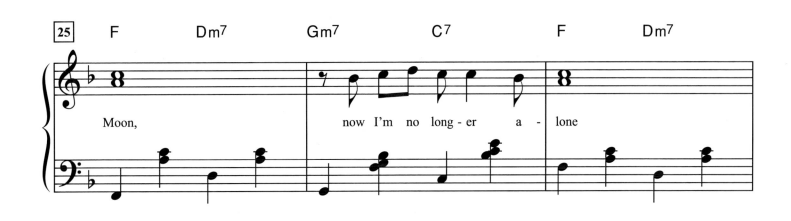

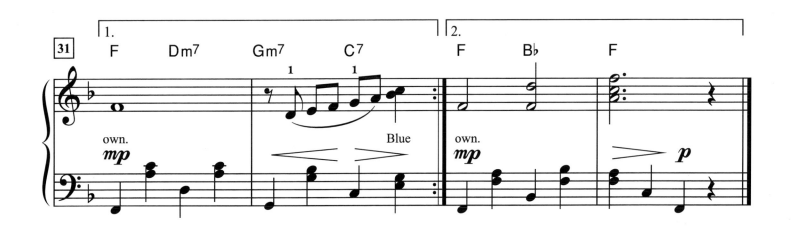

BREAKAWAY

Words and Music by
Matthew Gerrard, Bridget Benenate and Avril Lavigne
Arranged by Dan Coates

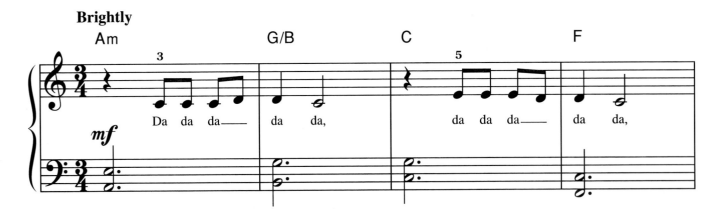

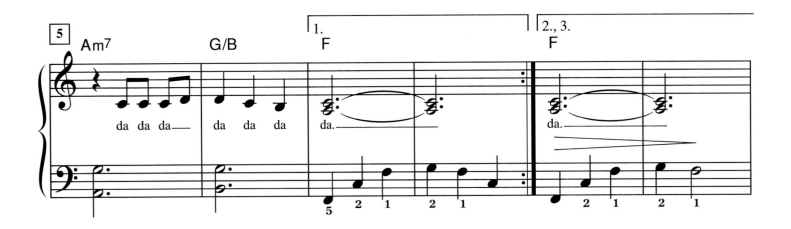

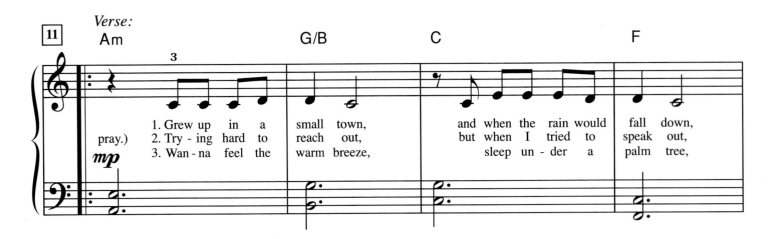

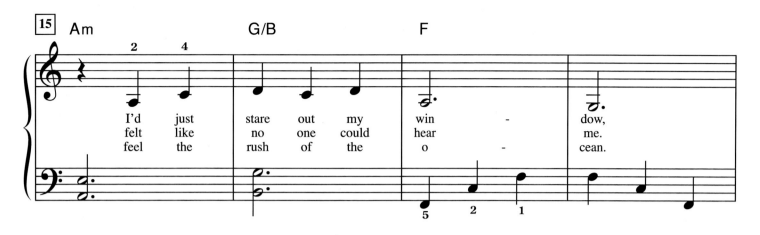

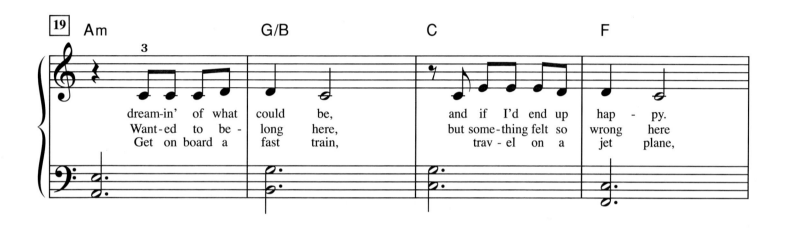

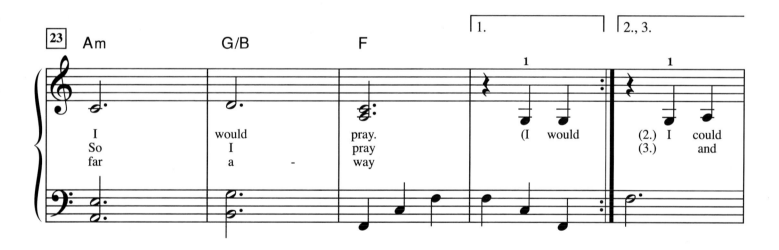

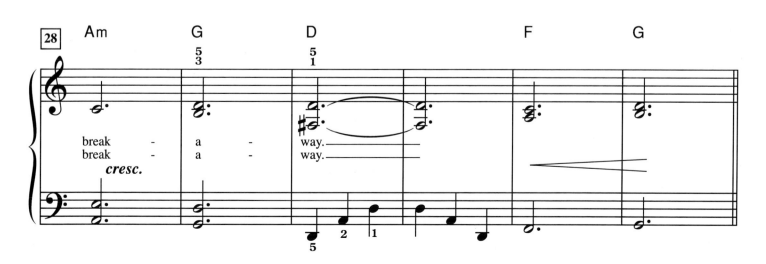

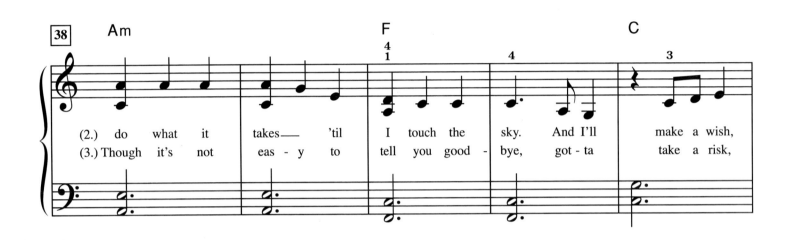

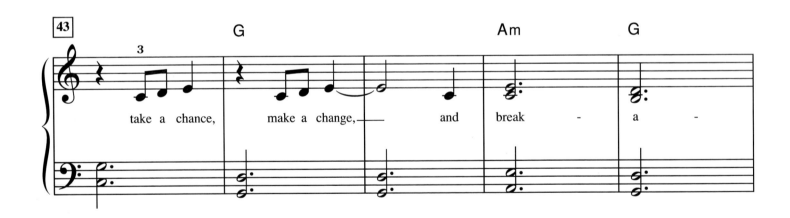

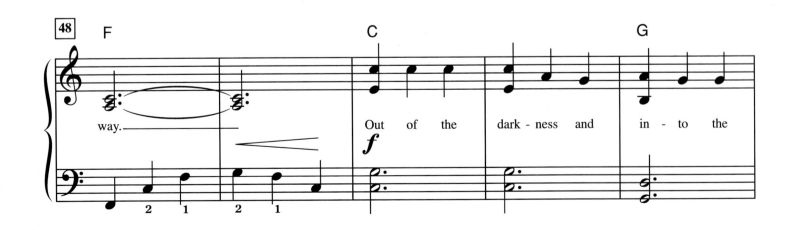

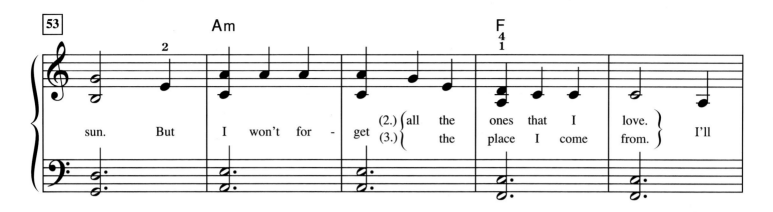

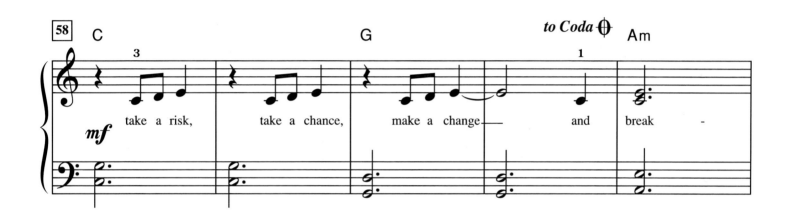

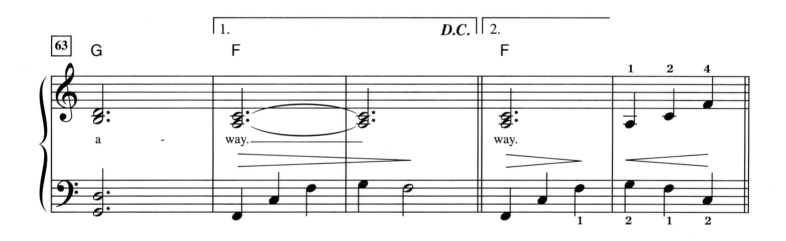

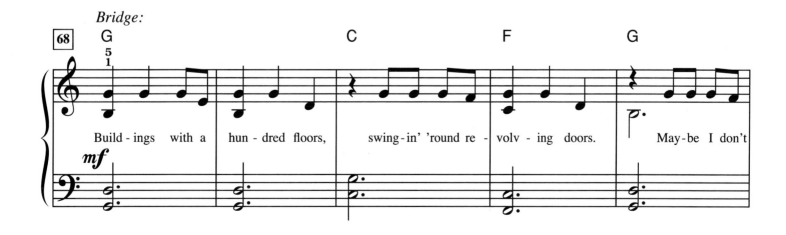

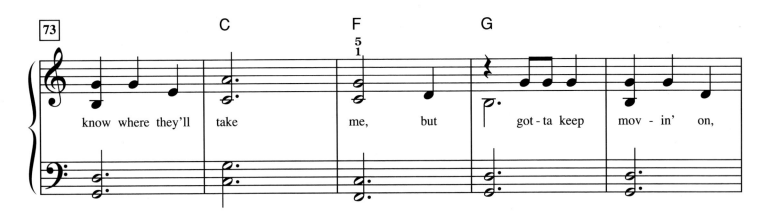

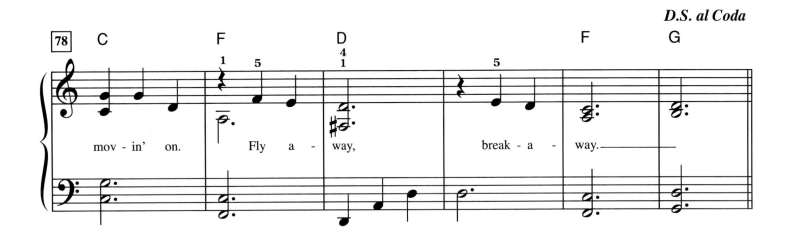

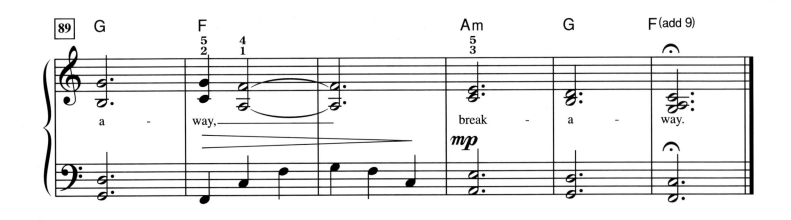

BYE BYE BLACKBIRD

Words by Mort Dixon
Music by Ray Henderson
Arranged by Dan Coates

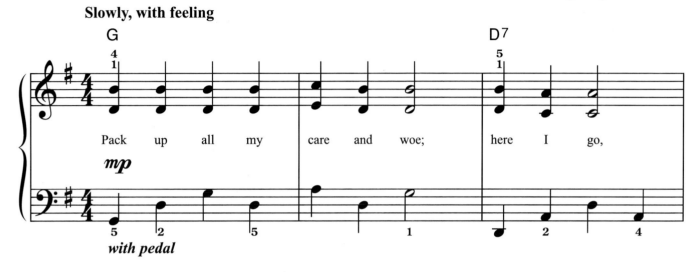

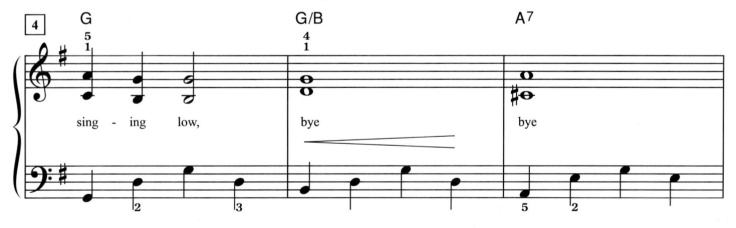

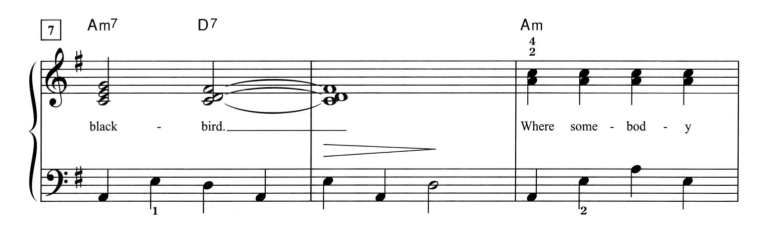

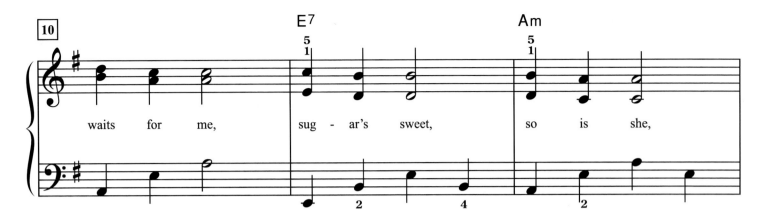

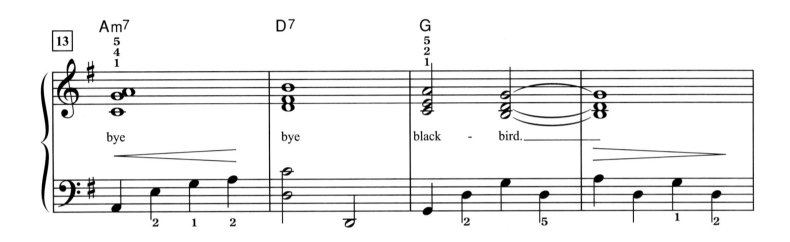

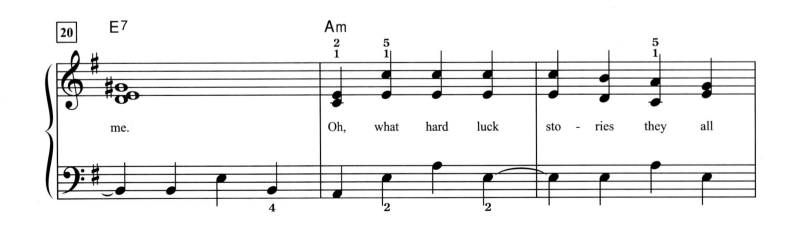

CELEBRATE ME HOME

Lyrics by Kenny Loggins
Music by Kenny Loggins and Bob James
Arranged by Dan Coates

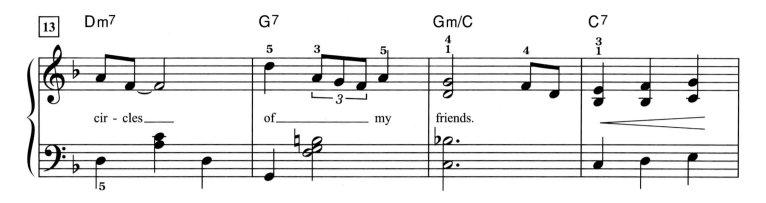

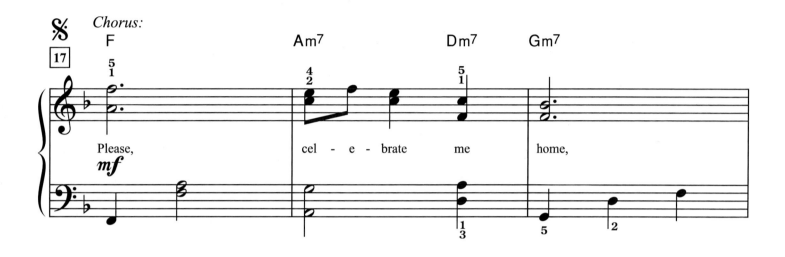

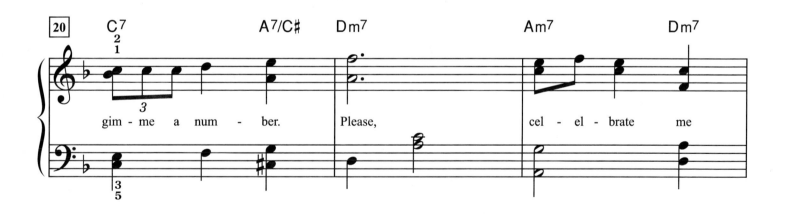

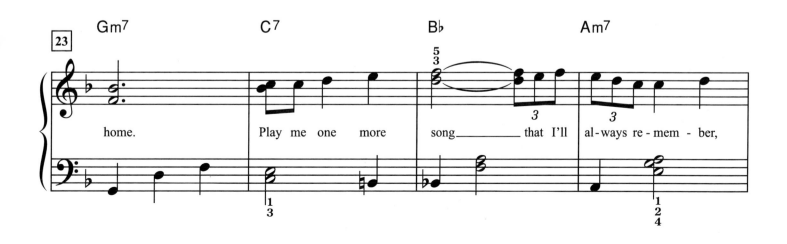

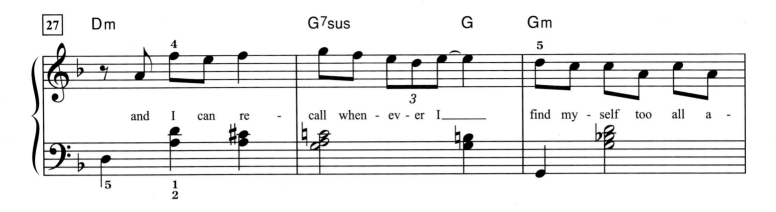

27 Dm   G⁷sus   G   Gm

and I can re - call when - ev - er I_____ find my - self too all a -

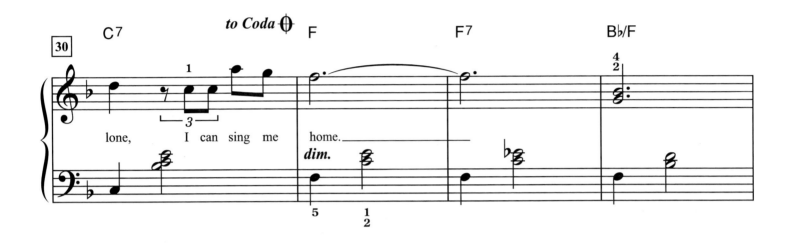

to Coda ⊕

30 C⁷   F   F⁷   B♭/F

lone, I can sing me home._____

dim.

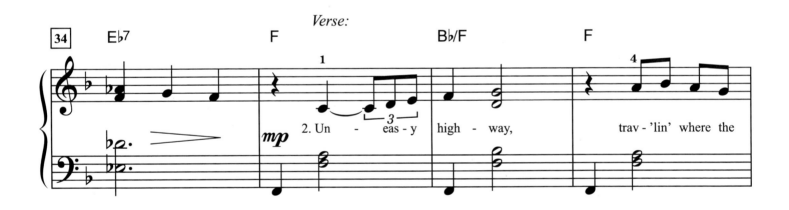

Verse:

34 E♭⁷   F   B♭/F   F

mp 2. Un - eas - y high - way, trav - 'lin' where the

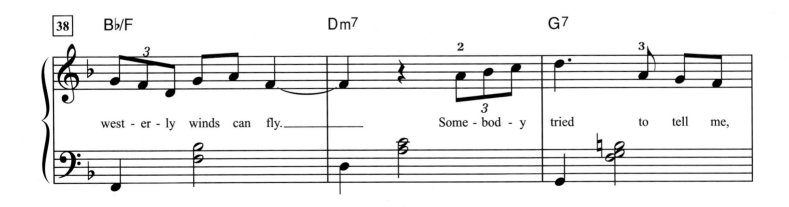

38 B♭/F   Dm⁷   G⁷

west - er - ly winds can fly._____ Some - bod - y tried to tell me,

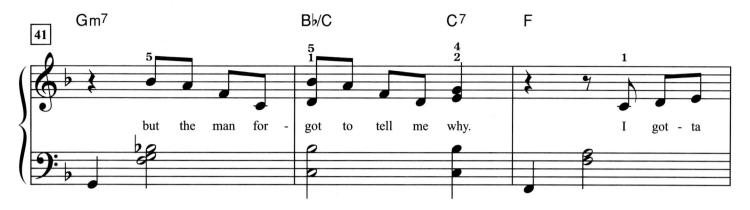

but the man for - got to tell me why.　　I got - ta

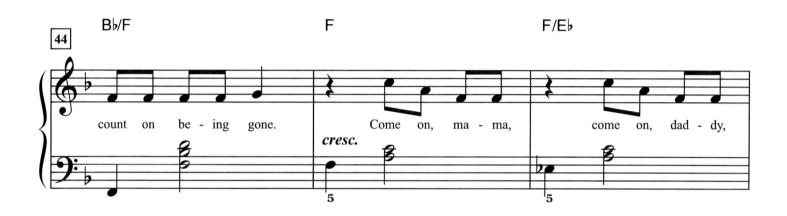

count on be - ing gone.　　Come on, ma - ma,　　come on, dad - dy,

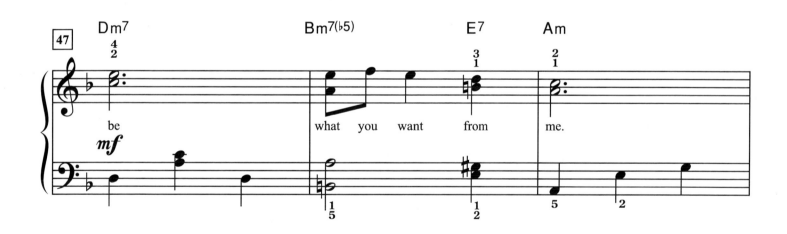

be　　what you want from　　me.

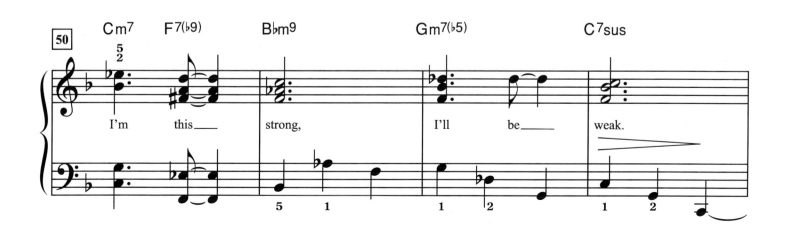

I'm this＿ strong,　　I'll be＿ weak.

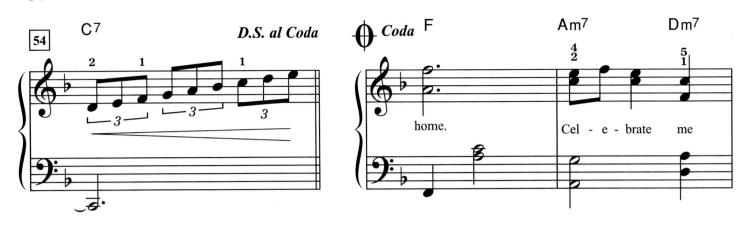

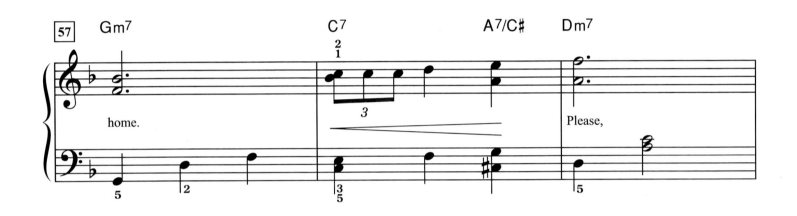

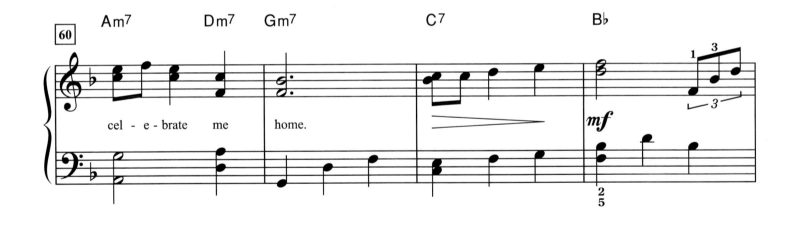

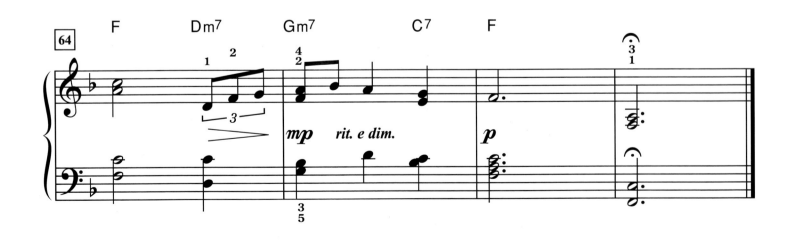

COME RAIN OR COME SHINE

Lyrics by Johnny Mercer
Music by Harold Arlen
Arranged by Dan Coates

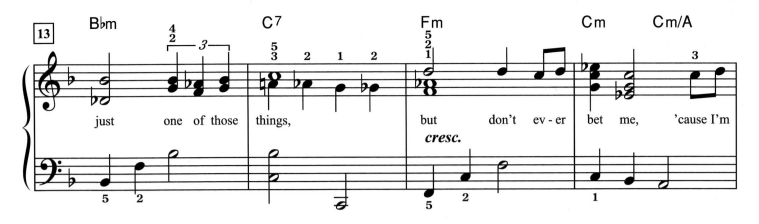

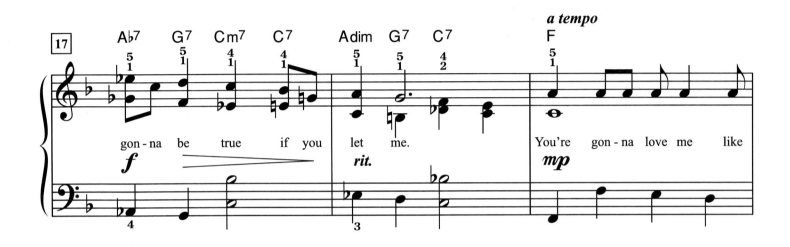

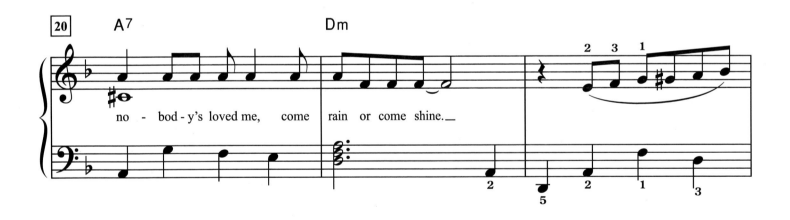

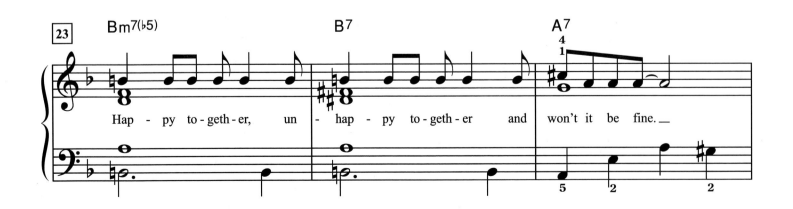

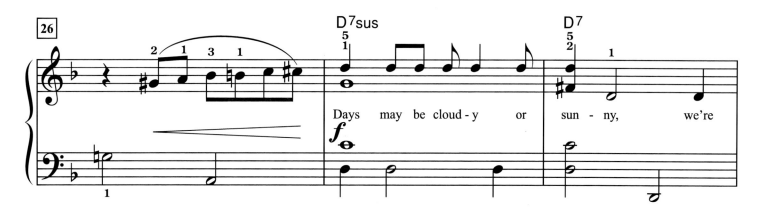

Days may be cloud-y or sun - ny, we're

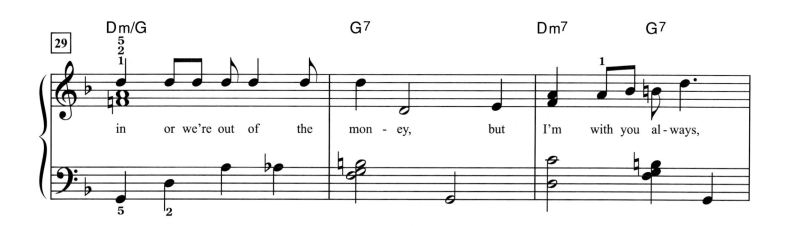

in or we're out of the mon - ey, but I'm with you al - ways,

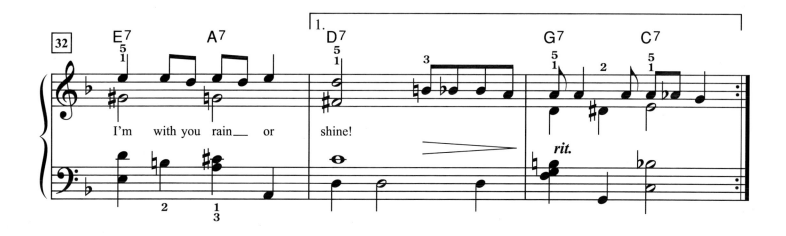

I'm with you rain __ or shine!

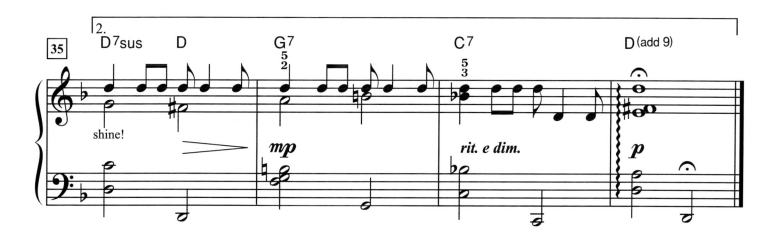

shine!

DESPERADO

Words and Music by
Don Henley and Glenn Frey
Arranged by Dan Coates

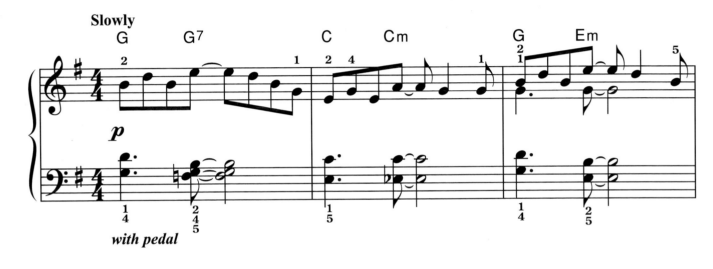

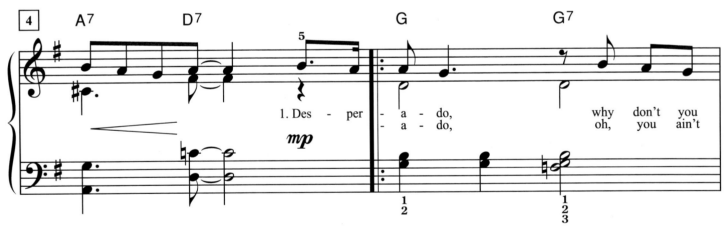

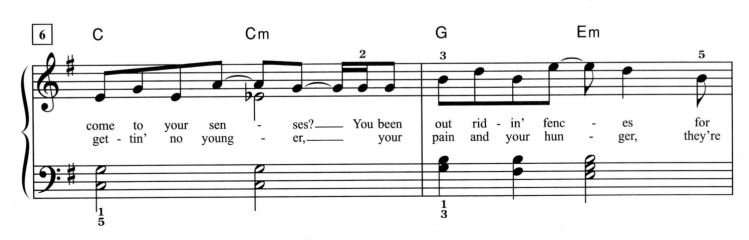

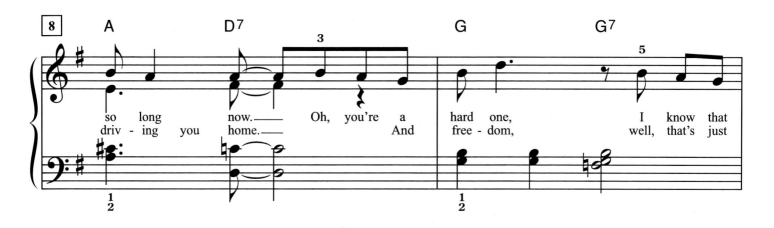

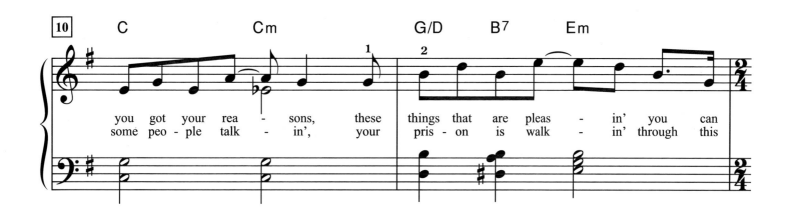

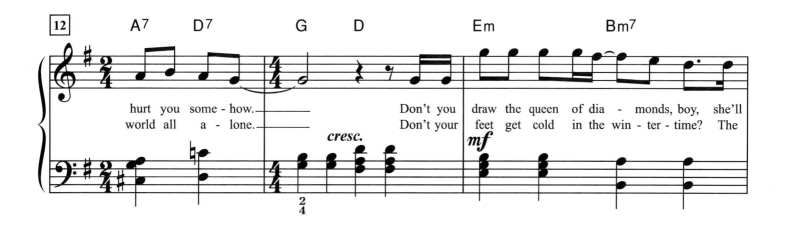

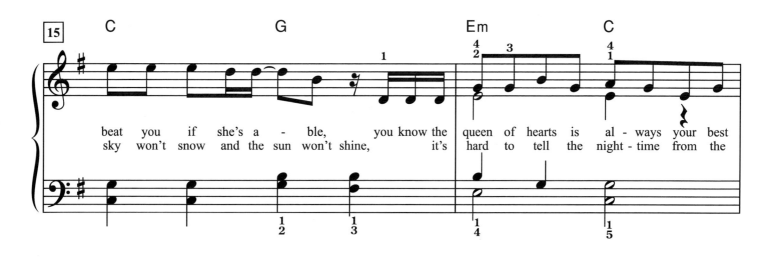

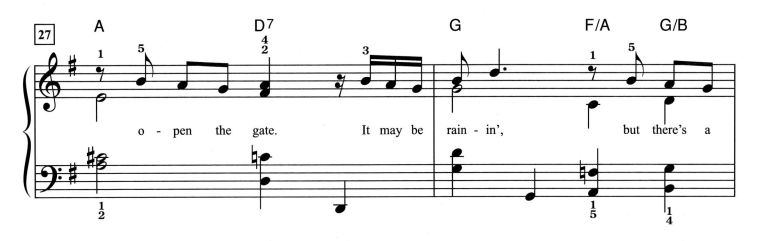

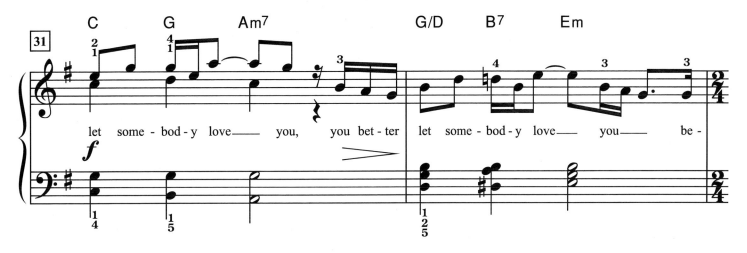

EVERYTHING

Words and Music by
Michael Bublé, Alan Chang and Amy Foster
Arranged by Dan Coates

Moderately, with a steady beat

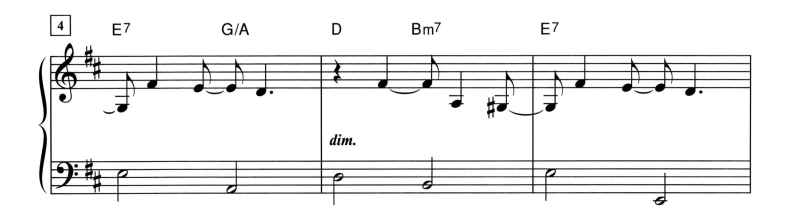

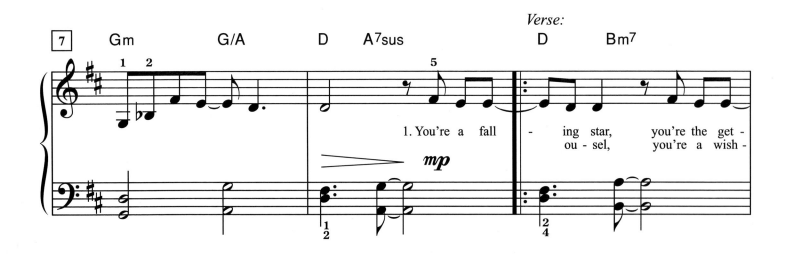

EARTH ANGEL (WILL YOU BE MINE)

Words and Music by Jesse Belvin
Arranged by Dan Coates

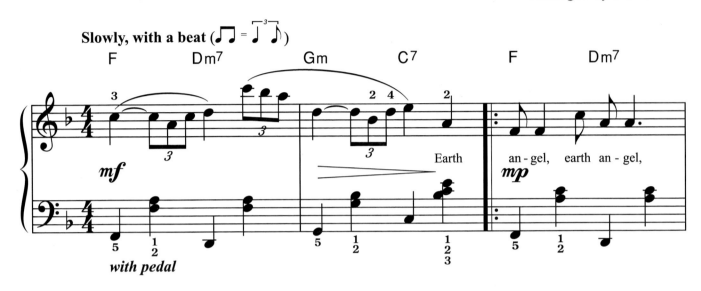

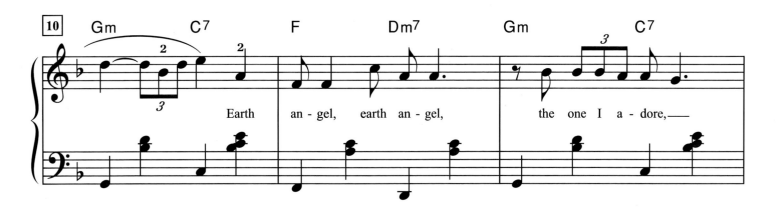

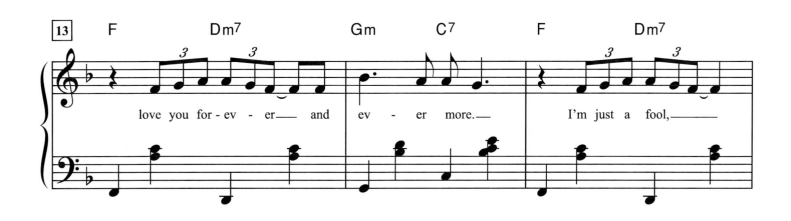

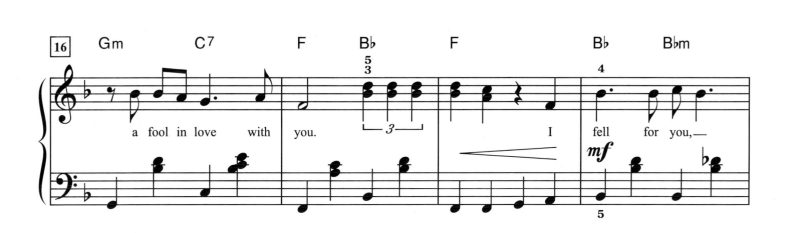

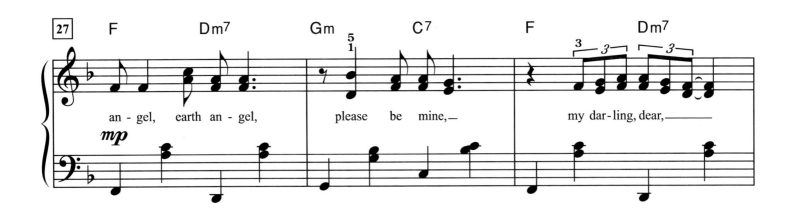

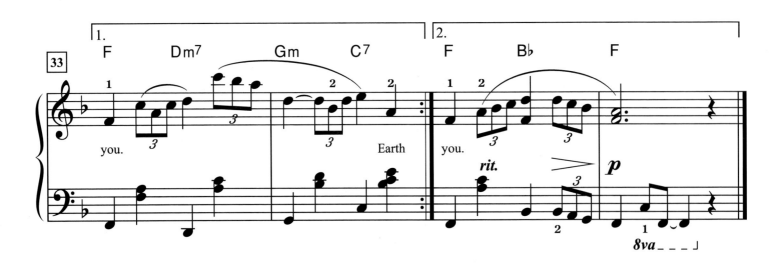

FALLING SLOWLY

(from *Once*)

Words and Music by
Glen Hansard and Marketa Irglova
Arranged by Dan Coates

Slowly, with expression

Verse:

1. I don't know you, but I want you all the more for
2. Fall - ing slow - ly, eyes that know me and I can't go

that. Words fall through me and al - ways fool me
back. Moods that take me and e - rase me

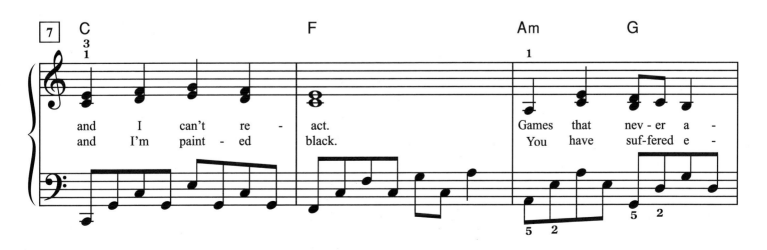

and I can't re - act. Games that nev - er a -
and I'm paint - ed black. You have suf - fered e -

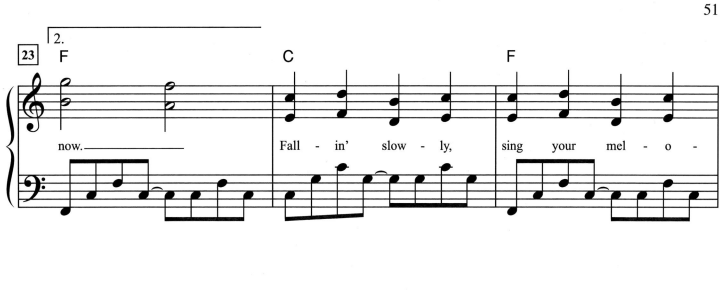

now._____ Fall - in' slow - ly, sing your mel - o -

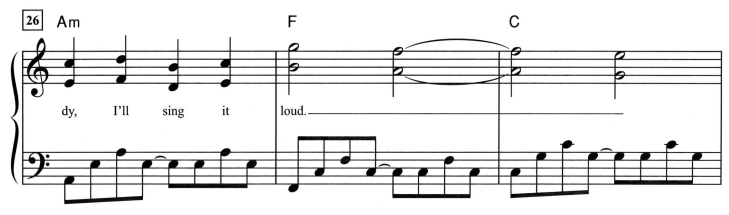

dy, I'll sing it loud._____

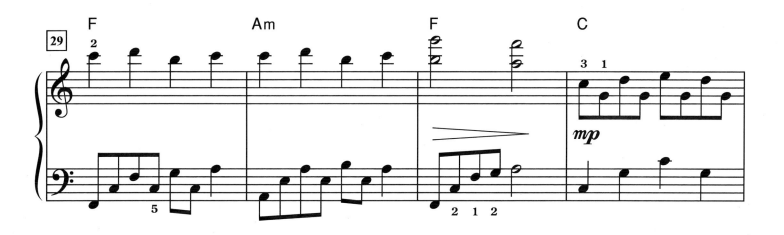

mp

dim.   *p*   *rit. e dim.*   *pp*

THE GREATEST LOVE OF ALL

Words by Linda Creed
Music by Michael Masser
Arranged by Dan Coates

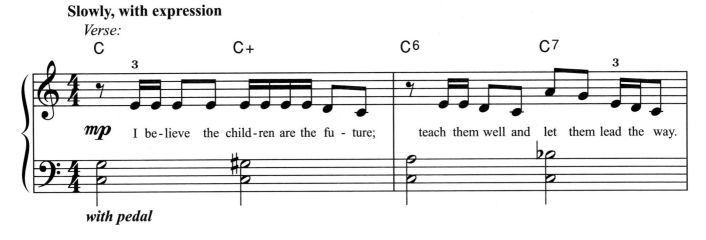

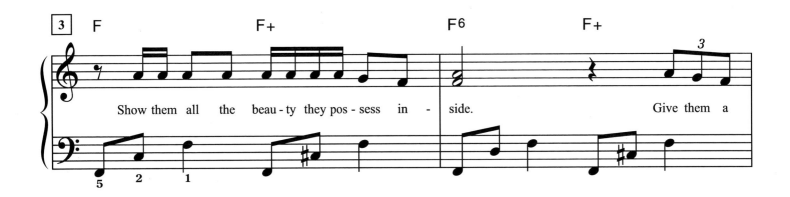

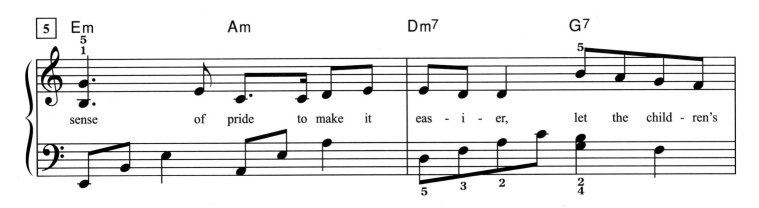

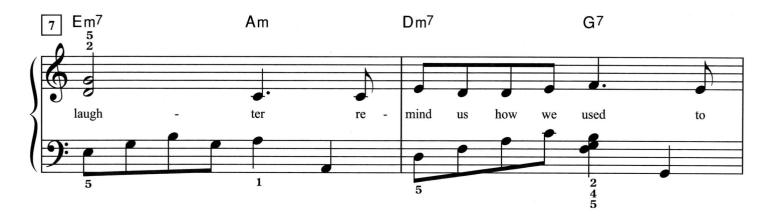

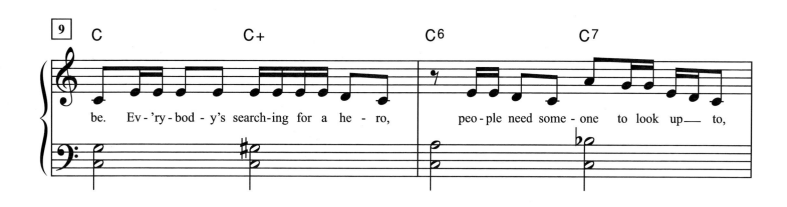

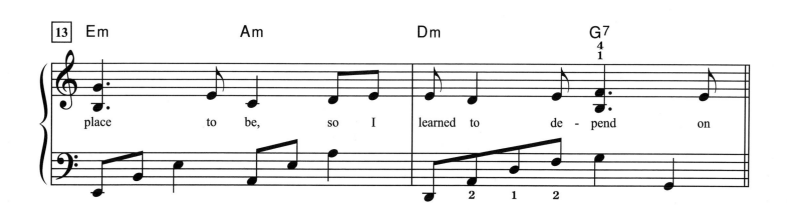

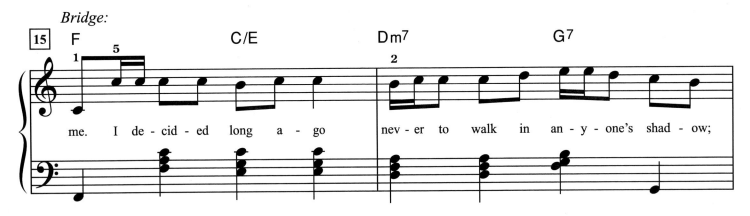

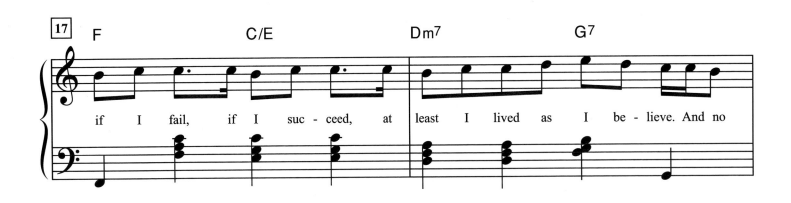

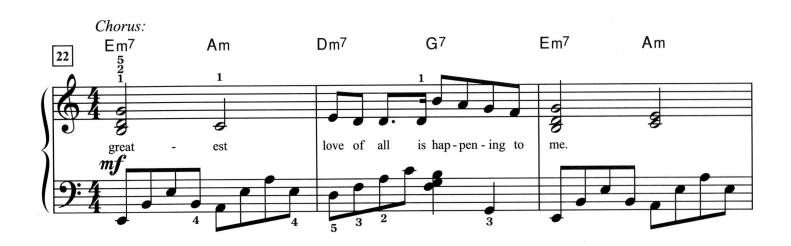

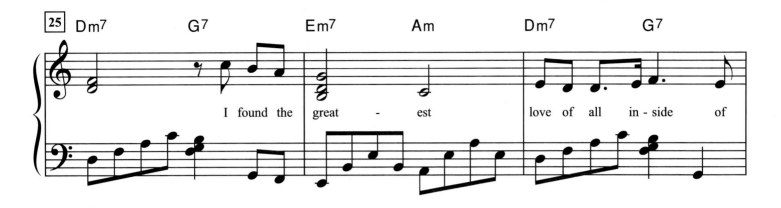

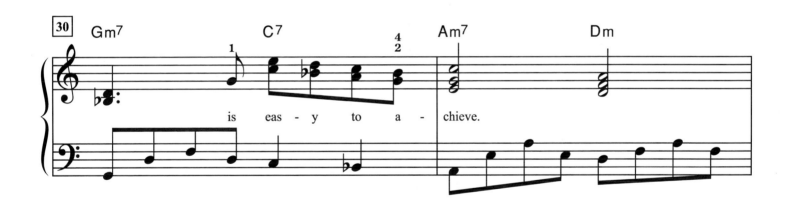

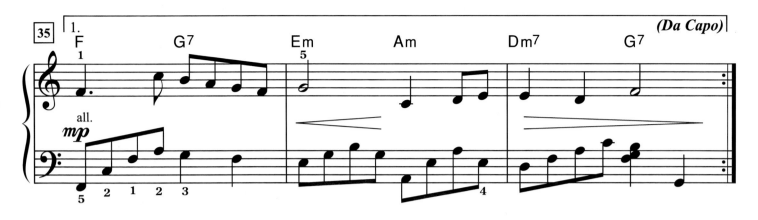

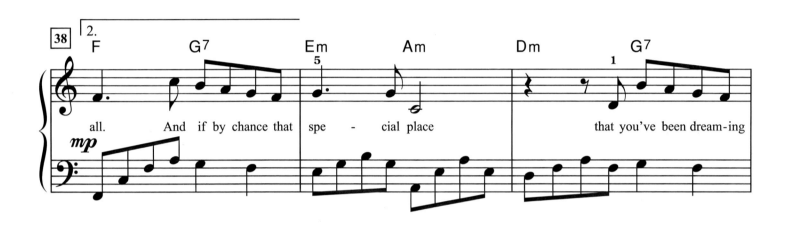

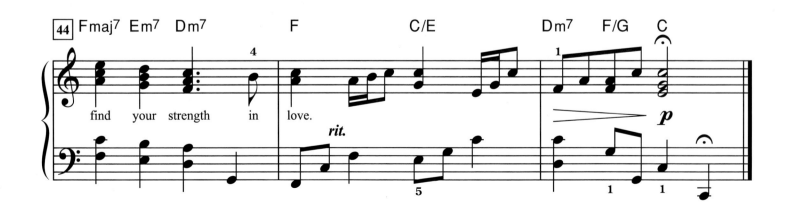

HEY THERE DELILAH

Words and Music by Tom Higgenson
Arranged by Dan Coates

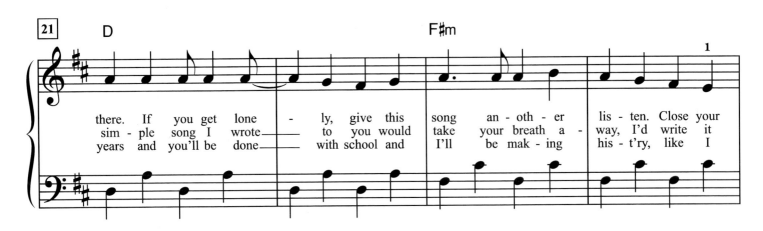

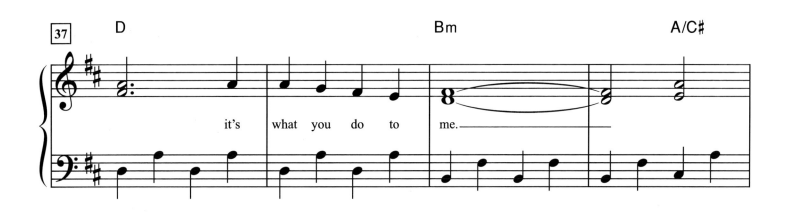

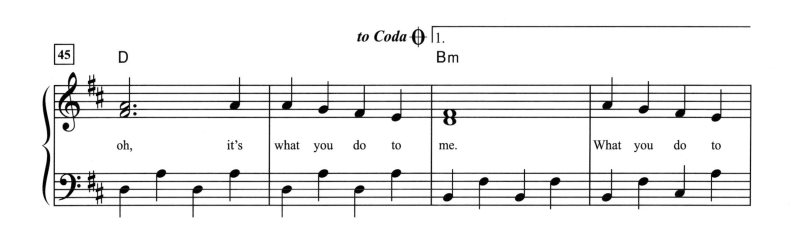

HEAL THE WORLD

Written and Composed by Michael Jackson
Arranged by Dan Coates

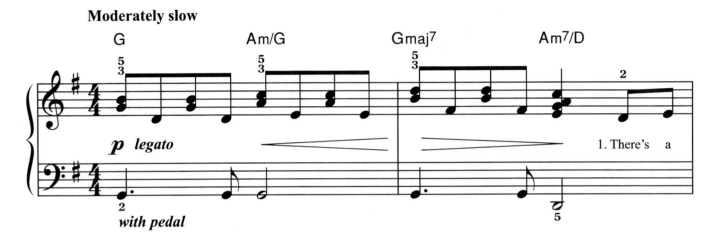

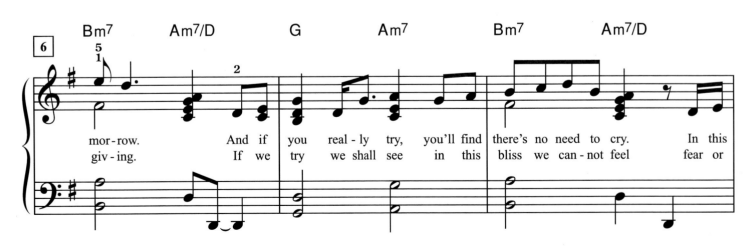

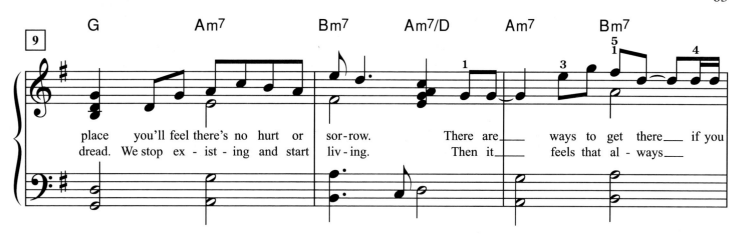

Chorus:

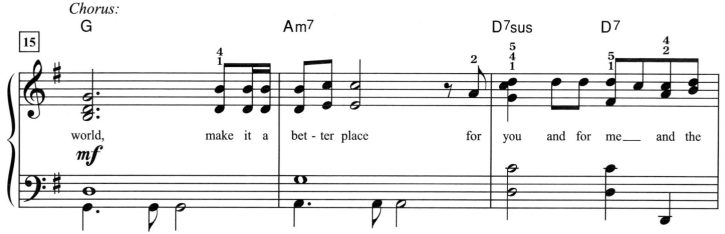

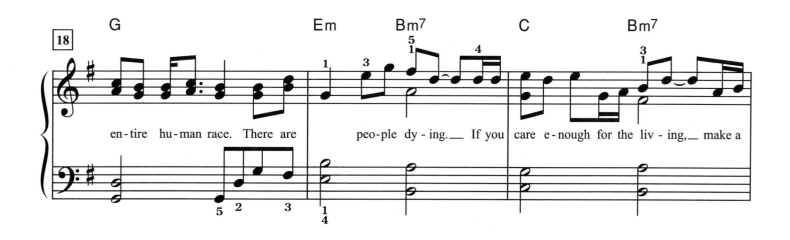

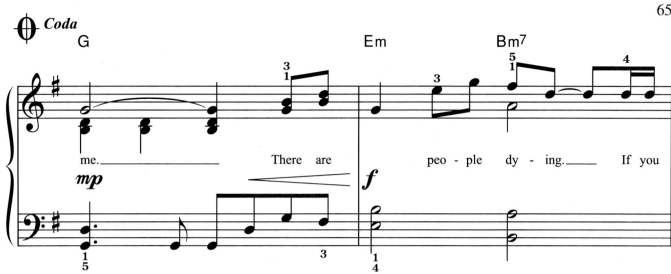

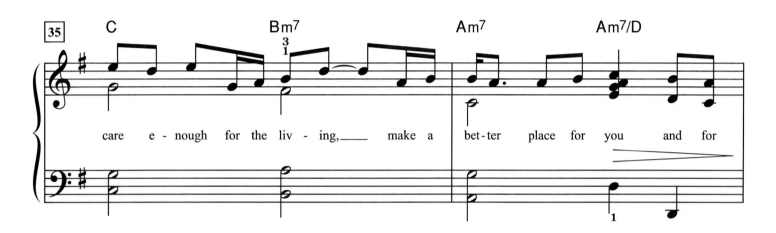

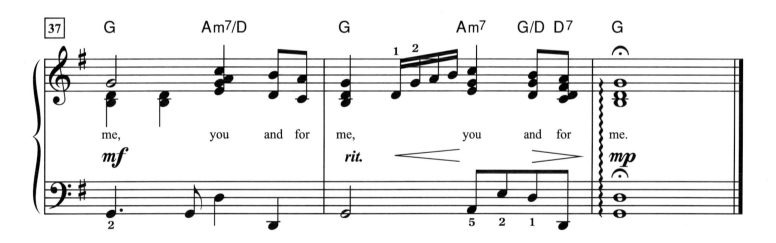

Verse 3:
We could fly so high,
Let our spirits never die.
In my heart, I feel you are all my brothers.
Create a world with no fear,
Together we cry happy tears.
See the nation turn their swords into plowshares.
We could really get there,
If you cared enough for the living.
Make a little space
To make a better place.
(To Chorus:)

HOW DEEP IS YOUR LOVE

Words and Music by
Barry Gibb, Maurice Gibb and Robin Gibb
Arranged by Dan Coates

Moderately, with a steady beat

HOW DO I LIVE

Words and Music by Diane Warren
Arranged by Dan Coates

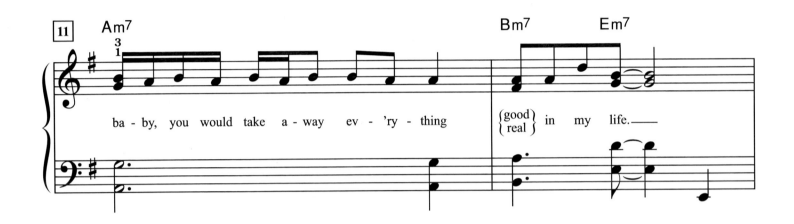

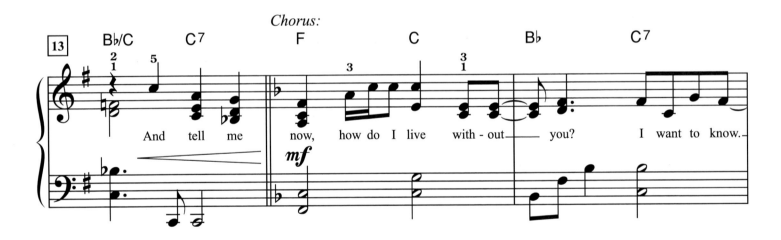

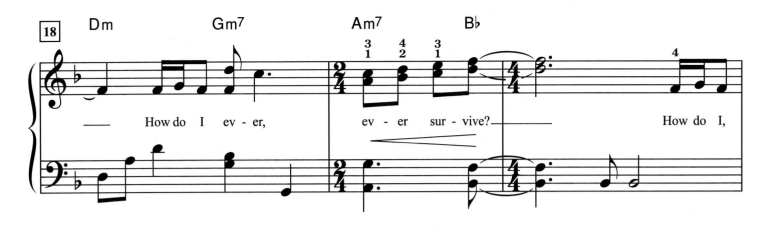

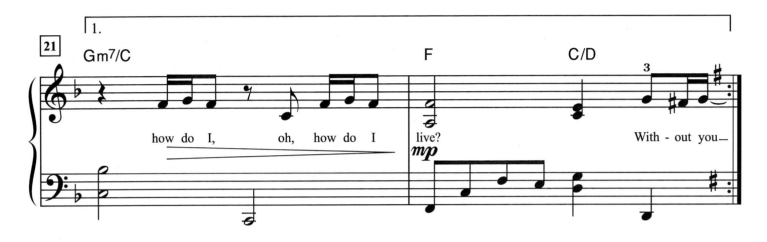

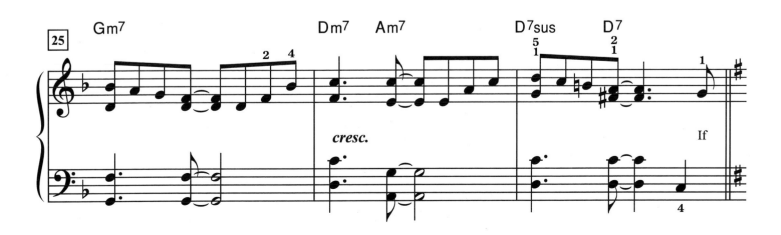

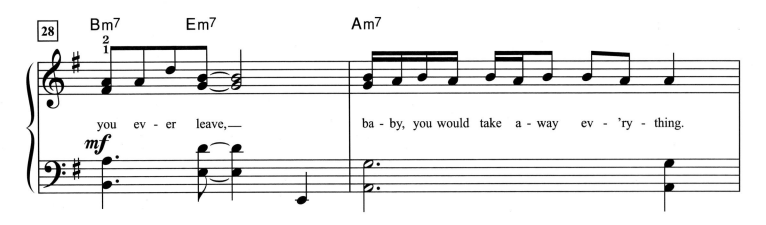

you ev - er leave,— ba - by, you would take a - way ev - 'ry - thing.

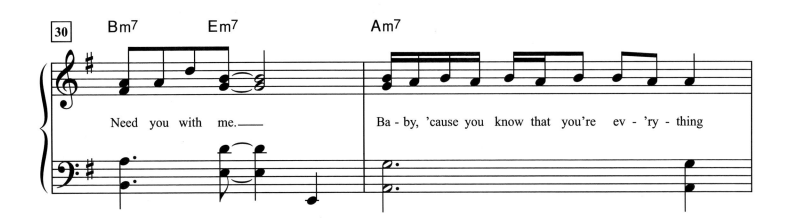

Need you with me.— Ba - by, 'cause you know that you're ev - 'ry - thing

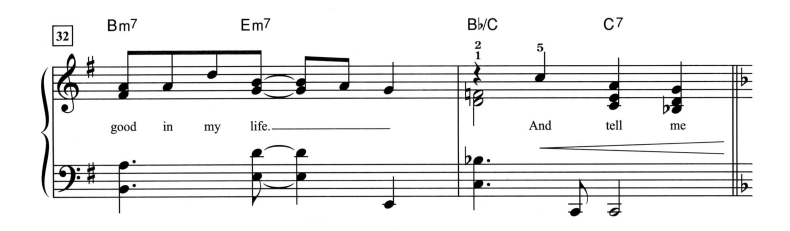

good in my life.— And tell me

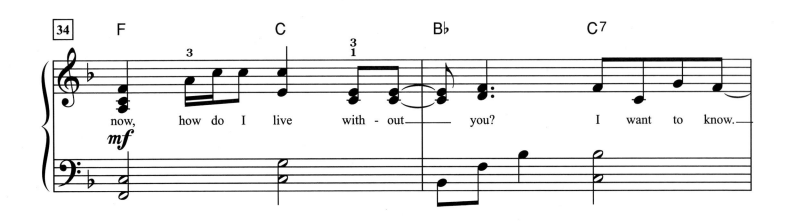

now, how do I live with - out— you? I want to know.—

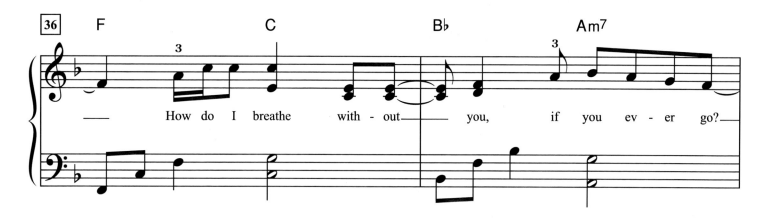

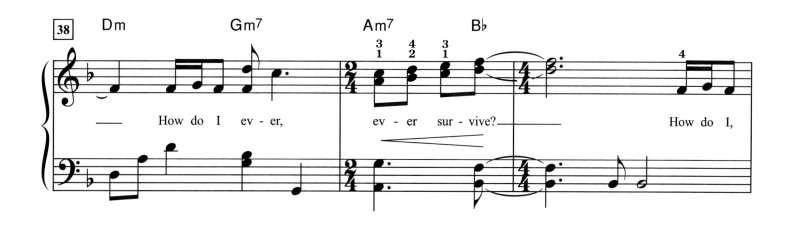

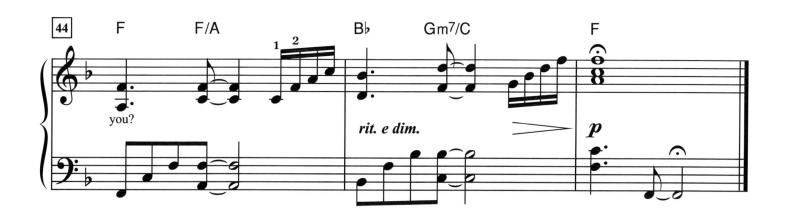

I DON'T WANT TO MISS A THING

(from *Armageddon*)

Words and Music by Diane Warren
Arranged by Dan Coates

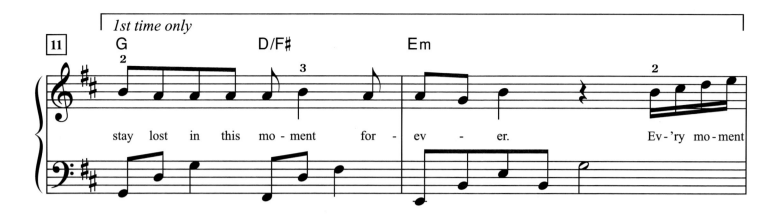

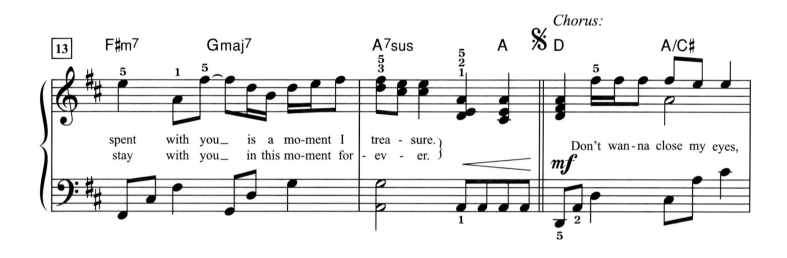

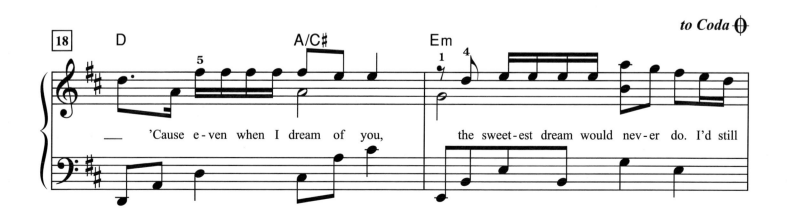

Bridge:

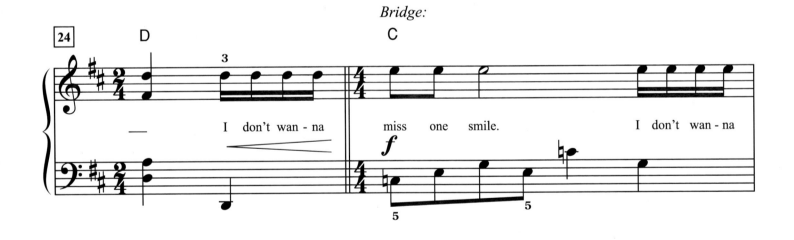

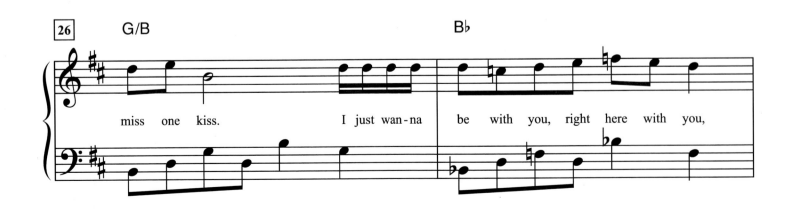

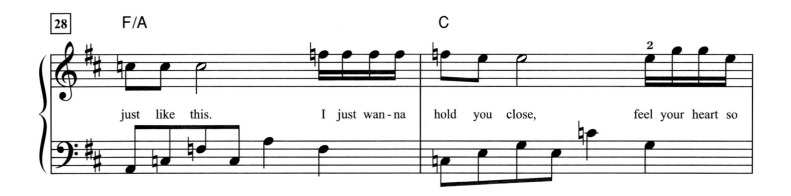

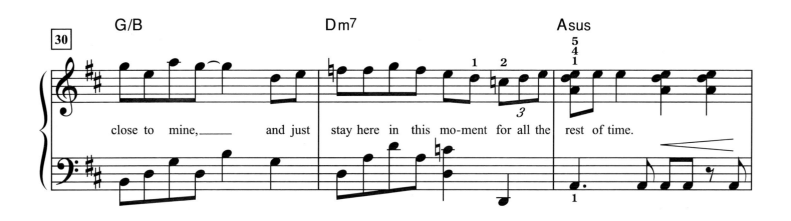

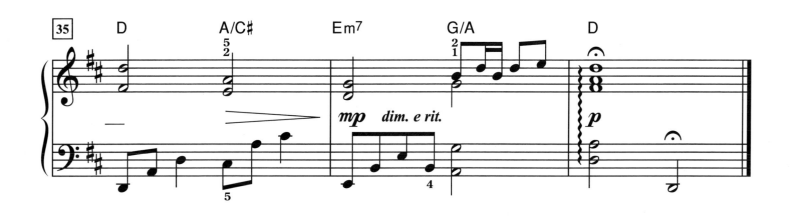

I KNEW I LOVED YOU

Lyrics by Alan and Marilyn Bergman
Music by Ennio Morricone
Arranged by Dan Coates

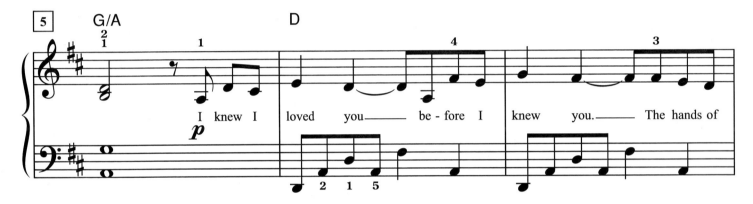

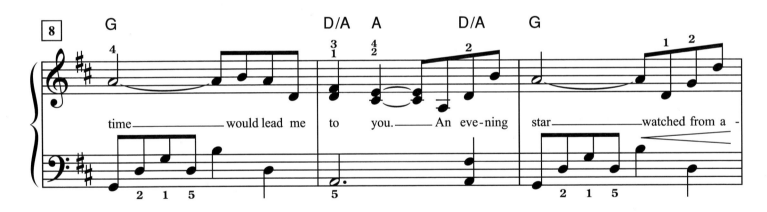

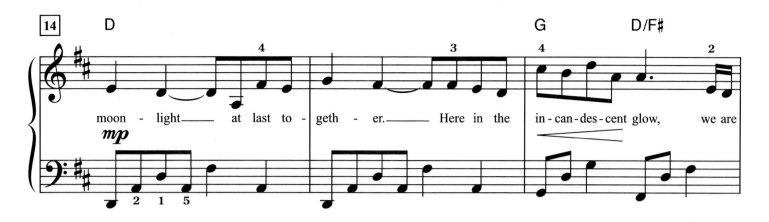

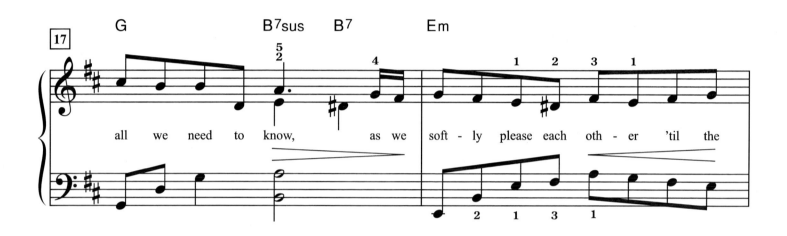

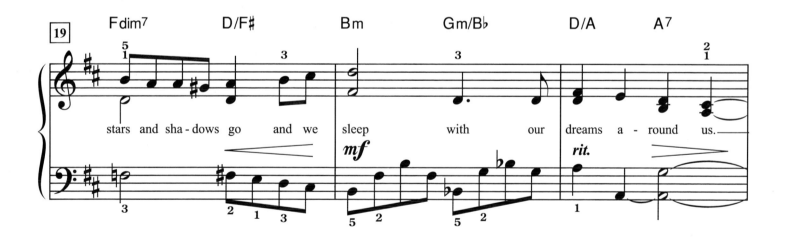

JAR OF HEARTS

Words and Music by
Drew Lawrence, Christina Perri and Barrett Yeretsian
Arranged by Dan Coates

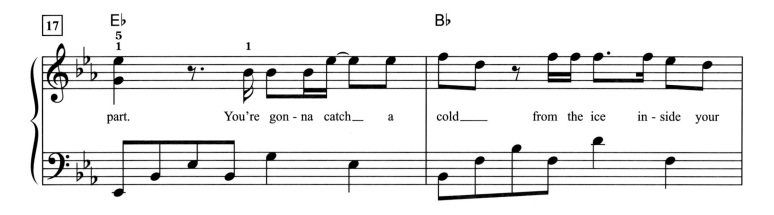

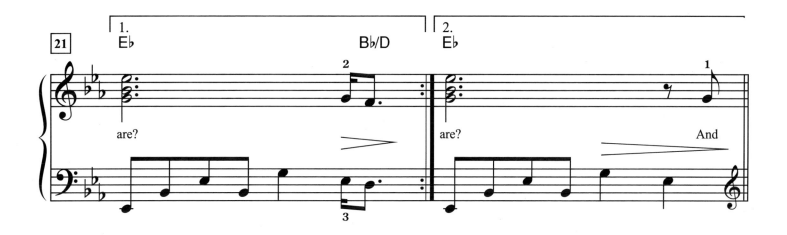

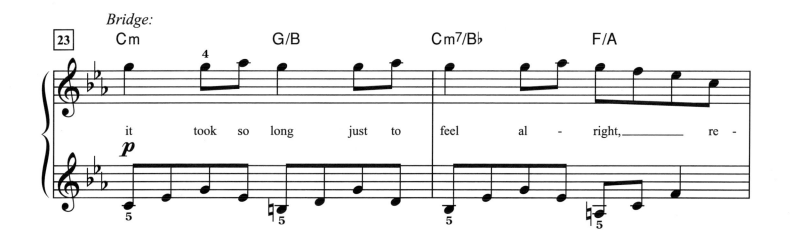

Verse 2:
I hear you're asking all around
If I am anywhere to be found.
But I have grown too strong
To ever fall back in your arms.
And I learned to live half alive,
And now you want me one more time.
(To Chorus:)

KILLING ME SOFTLY

Words and Music by
Charles Fox and Norman Gimbel
Arranged by Dan Coates

LA VIE EN ROSE

(Take Me to Your Heart Again)

Original French Lyrics By Edith Piaf
Music by Luis Guglielmi
English Lyrics by Mack David
Arranged by Dan Coates

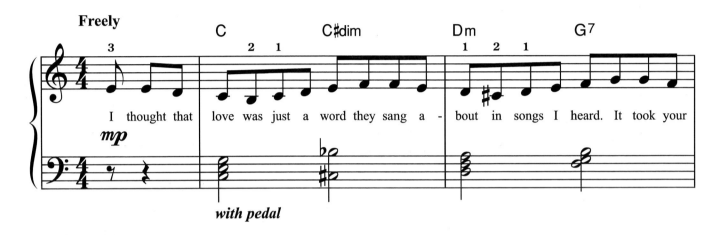

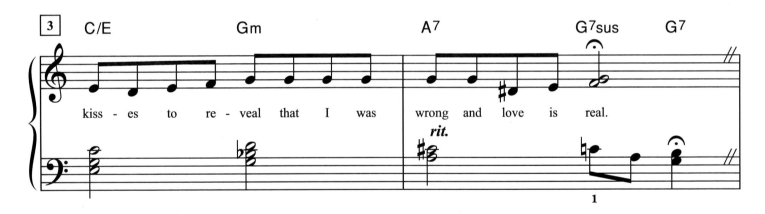

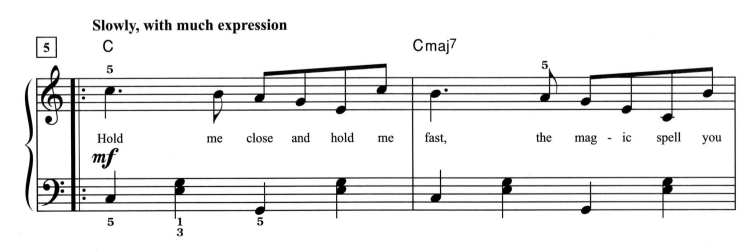

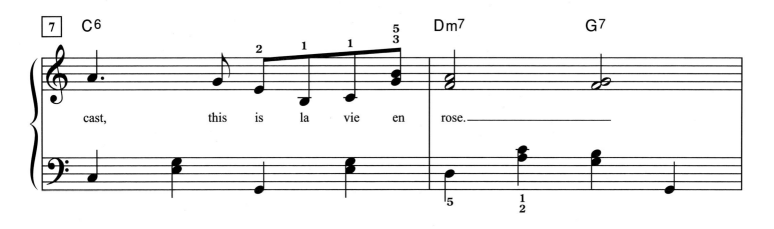

cast, this is la vie en rose.

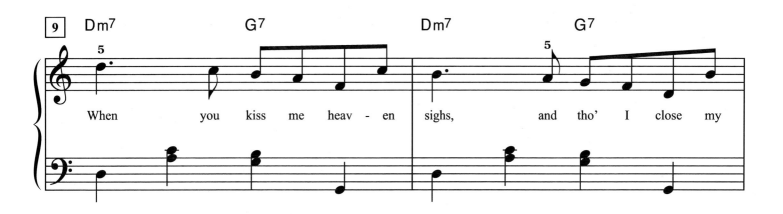

When you kiss me heav - en sighs, and tho' I close my

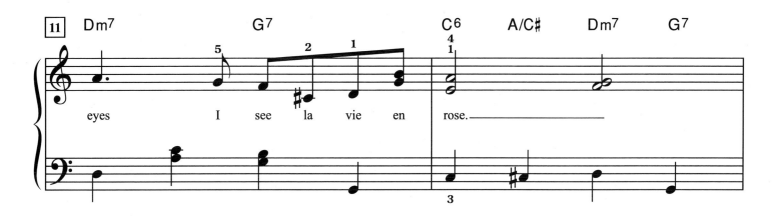

eyes I see la vie en rose.

When you press me to your heart I'm in a world a -

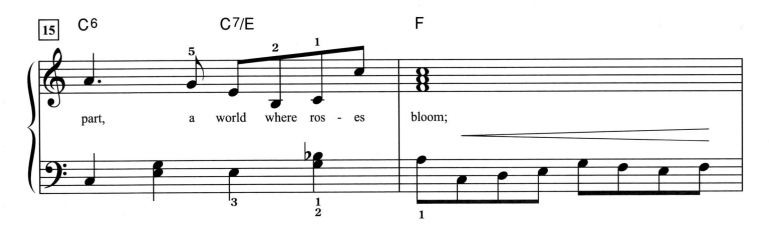

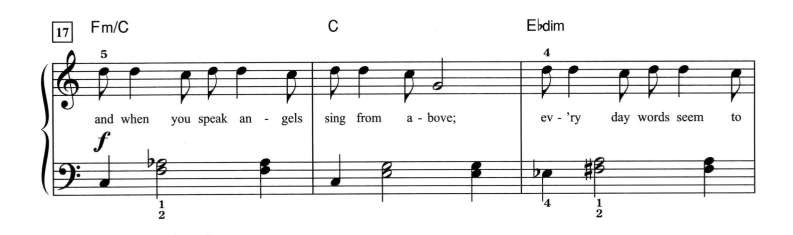

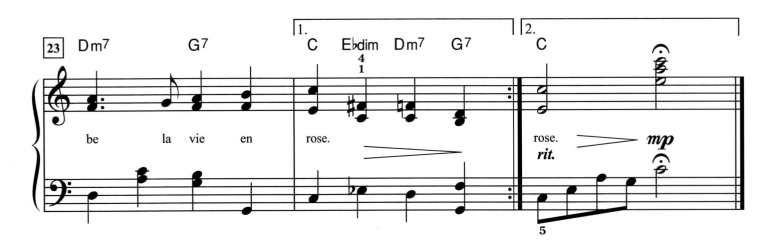

LAURA

Lyrics by Johnny Mercer
Music by David Raksin
Arranged by Dan Coates

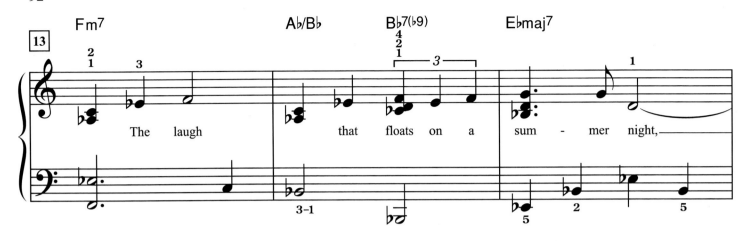

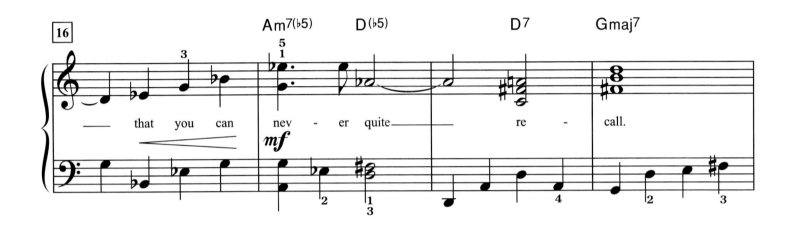

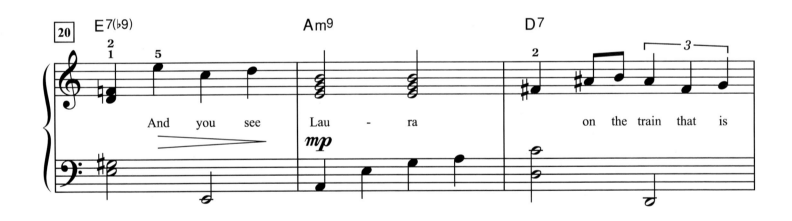

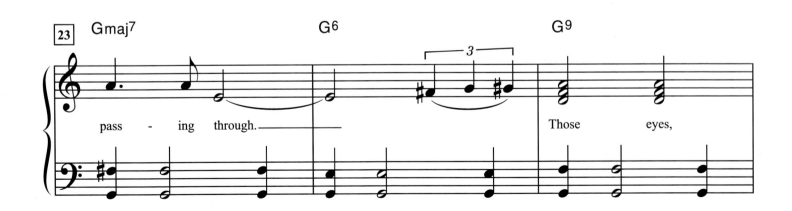

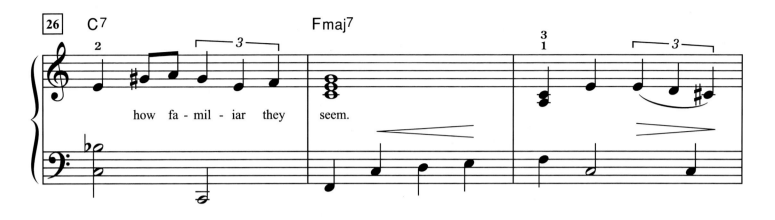

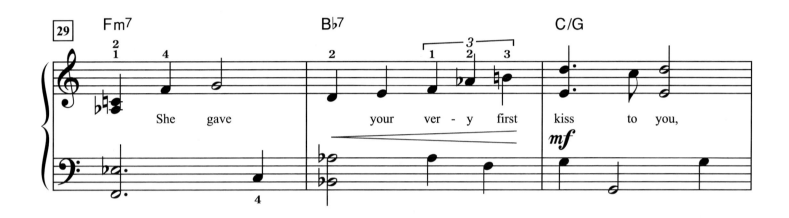

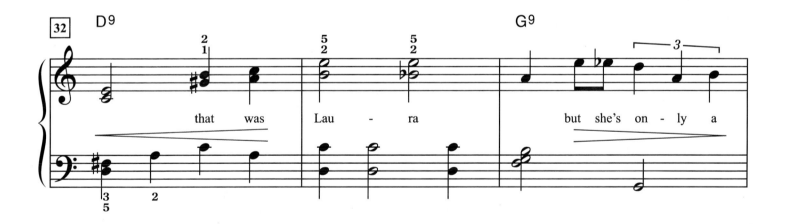

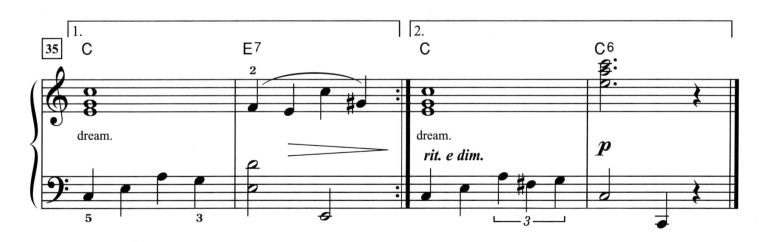

LOST

Words and Music by
Michael Bublé, Alan Chang and Jann Arden
Arranged by Dan Coates

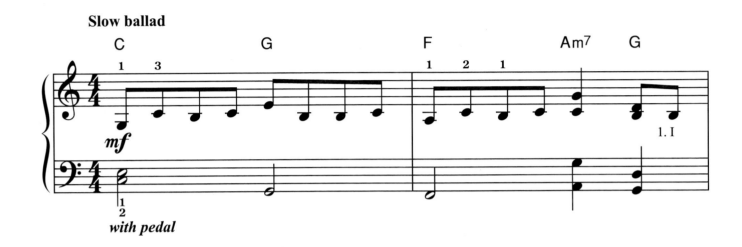

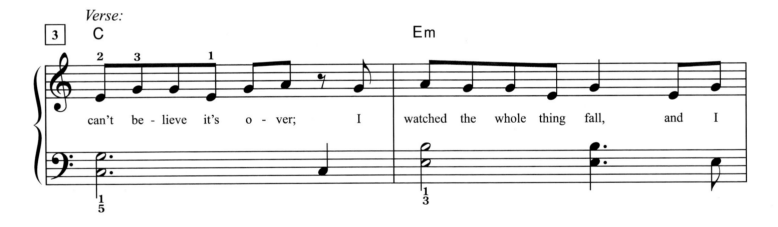

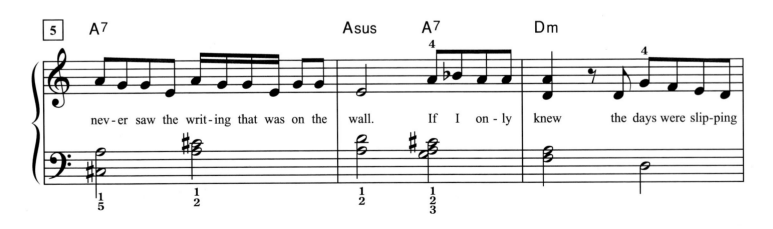

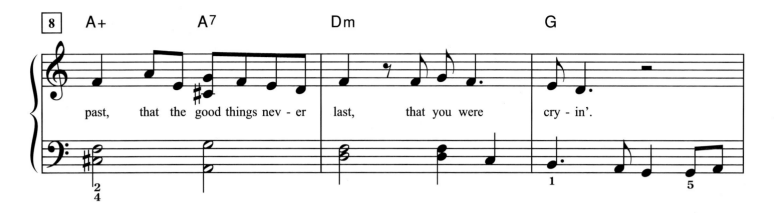

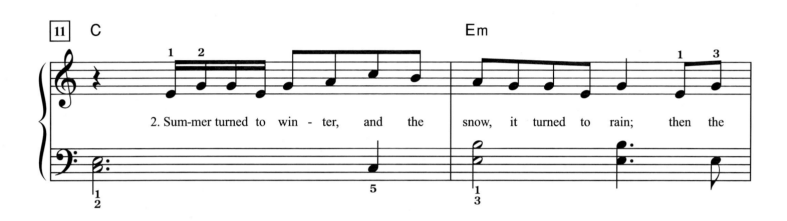

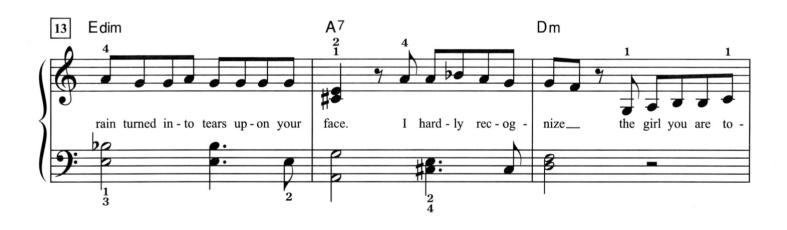

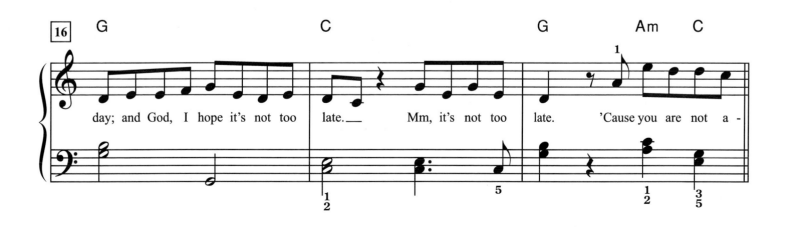

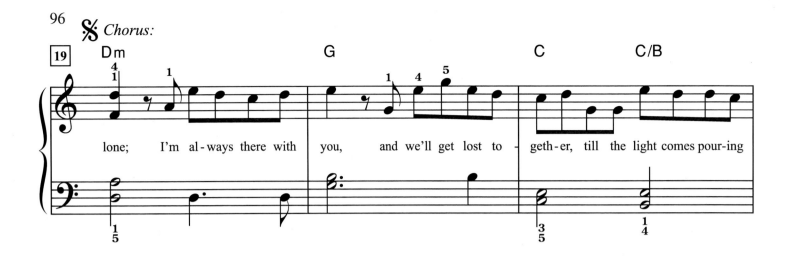

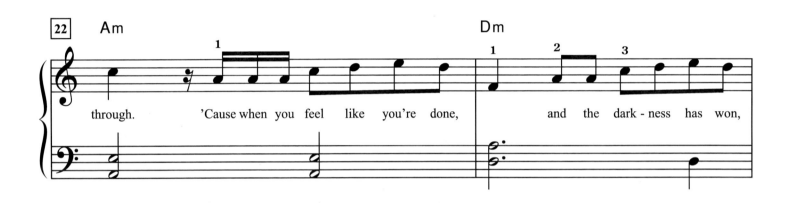

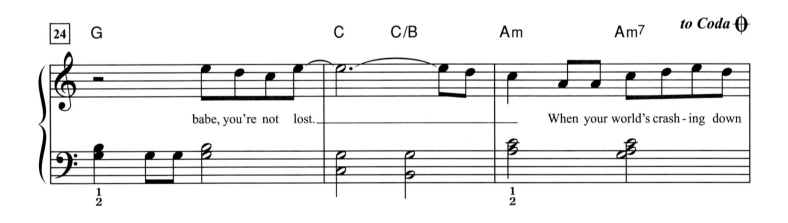

Verse:

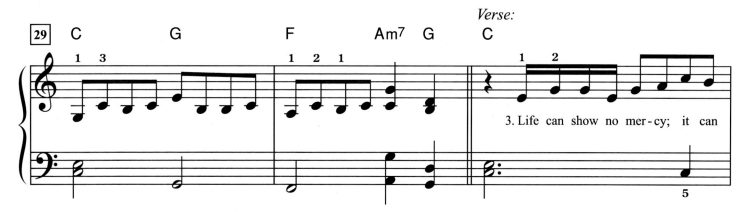

29 C G F Am7 G C

3. Life can show no mer-cy; it can

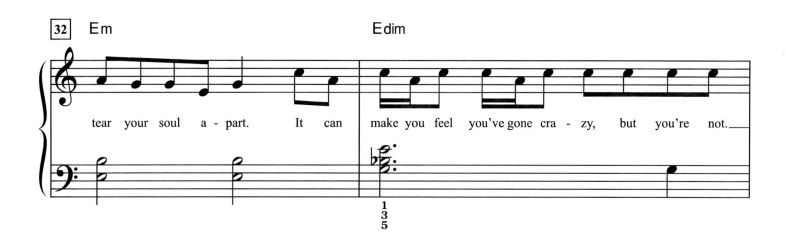

32 Em Edim

tear your soul a - part. It can make you feel you've gone cra - zy, but you're not.___

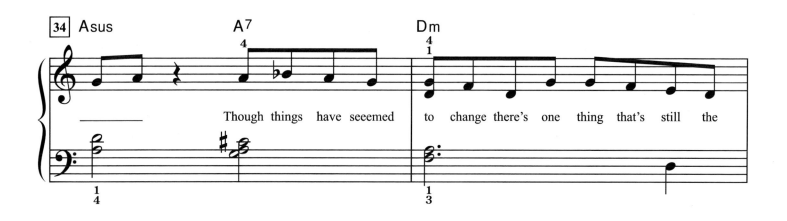

34 Asus A7 Dm

___ Though things have seeemed to change there's one thing that's still the

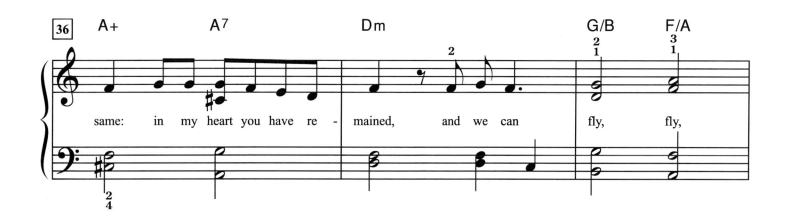

36 A+ A7 Dm G/B F/A

same: in my heart you have re - mained, and we can fly, fly,

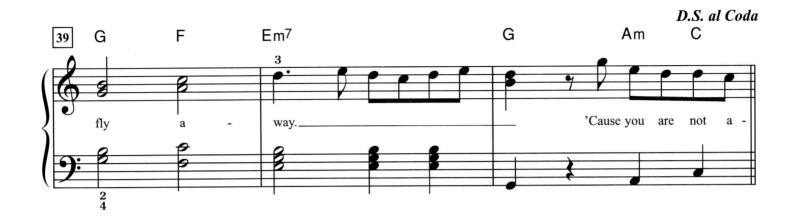

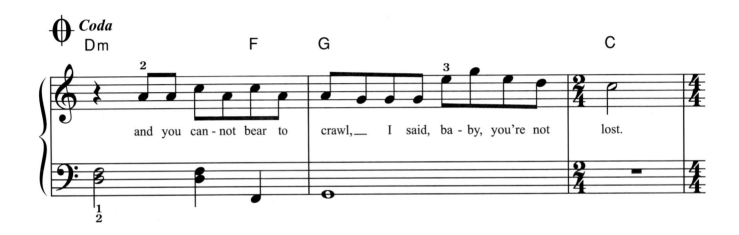

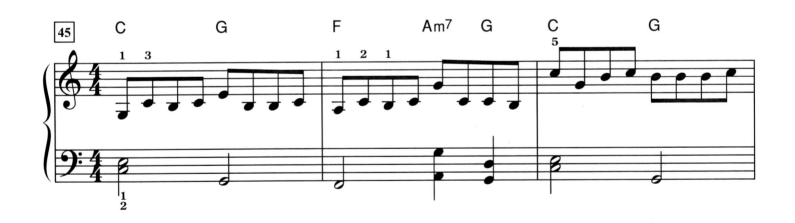

LOVE WILL LEAD YOU BACK

Words and Music by Diane Warren
Arranged by Dan Coates

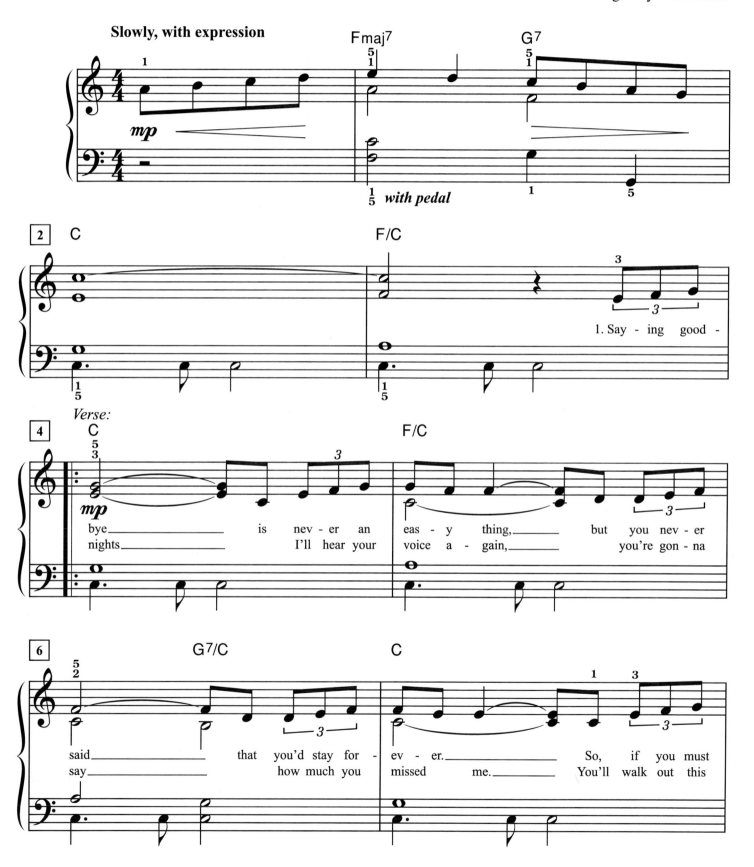

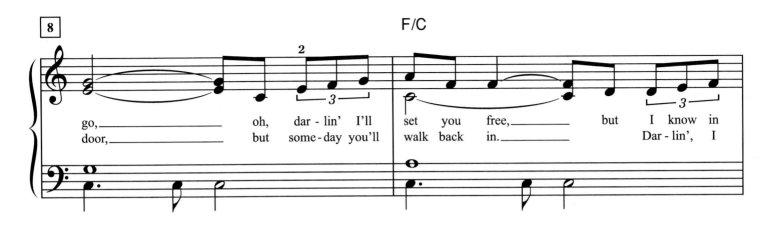

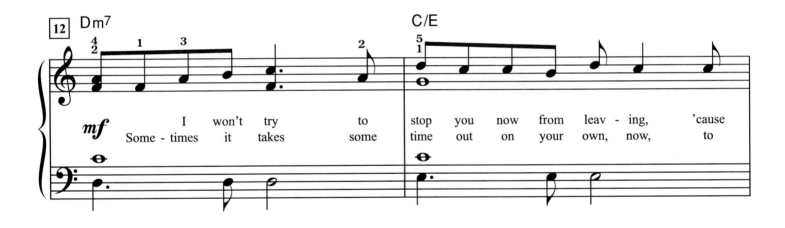

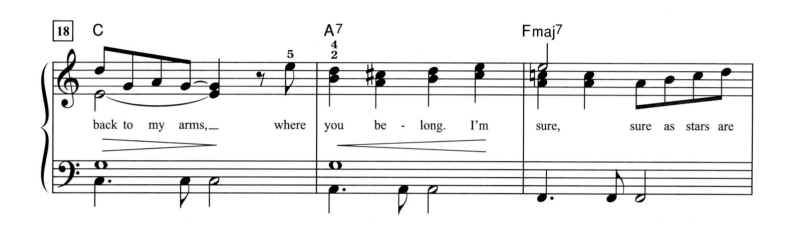

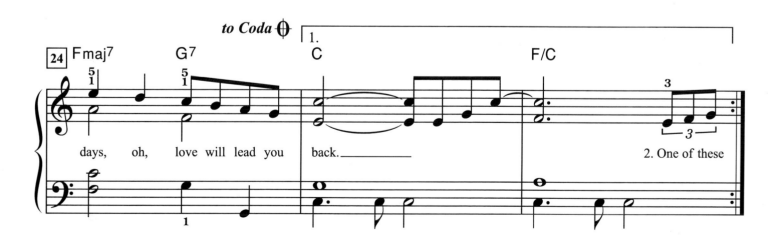

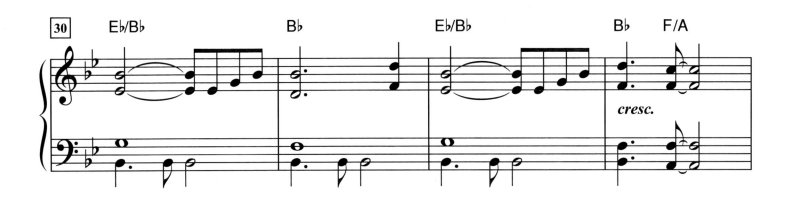

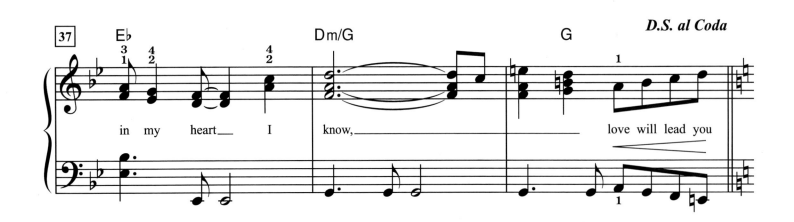

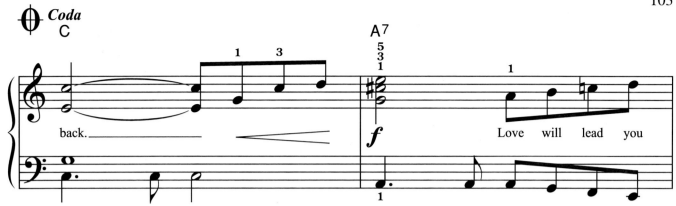

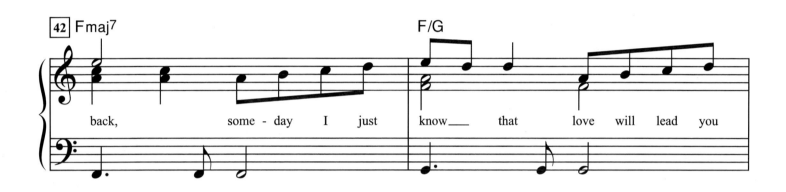

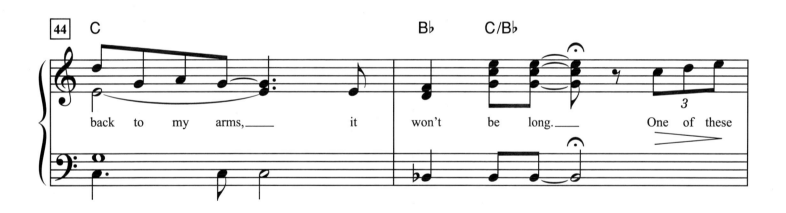

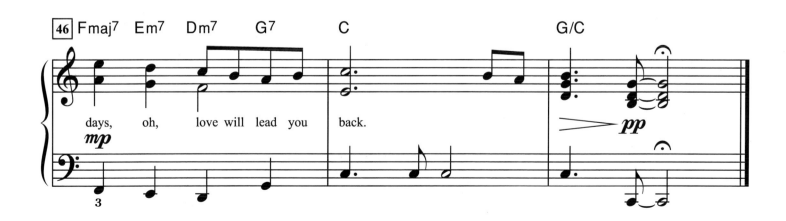

MISTY

Music by Erroll Garner
Arranged by Dan Coates

Slowly, with expression

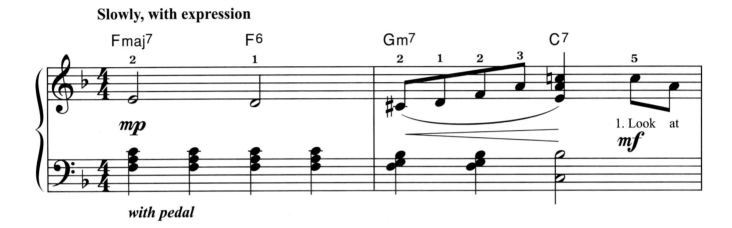

1. Look at

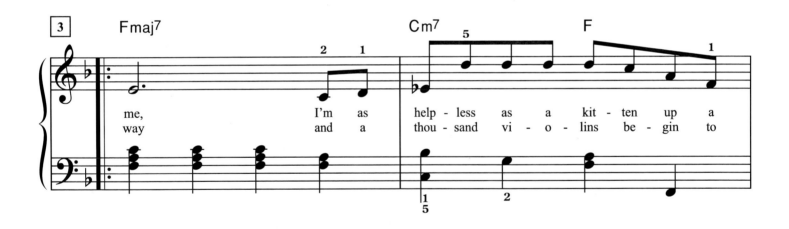

me,   I'm as   help - less as a kit - ten up a
way   and a   thou - sand vi - o - lins be - gin to

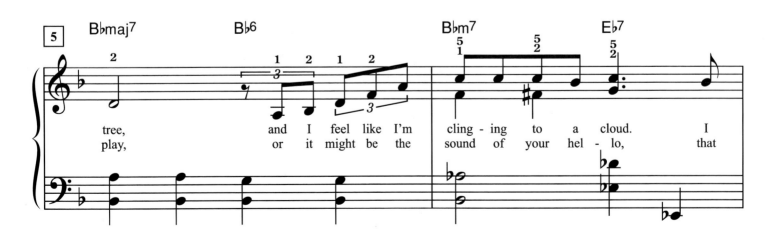

tree,   and I feel like I'm   cling - ing to a cloud.   I
play,   or it might be the   sound of your hel - lo,   that

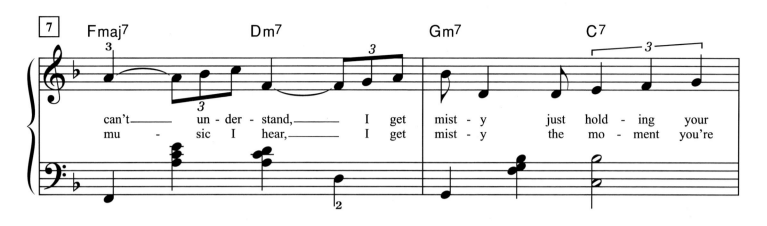

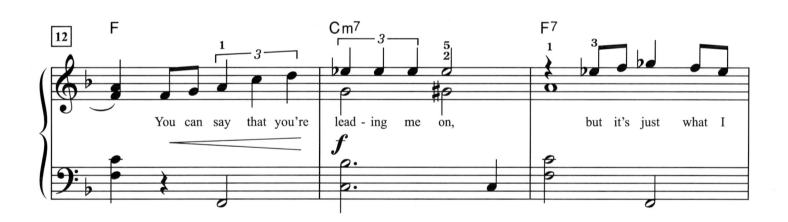

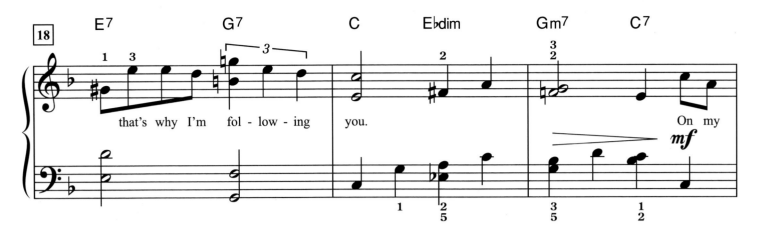

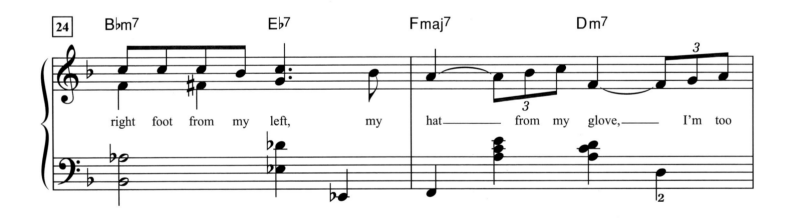

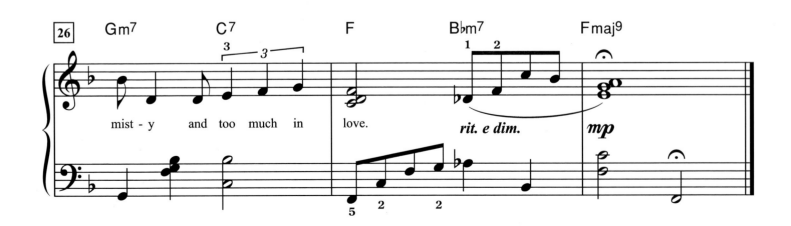

NIGHT AND DAY

(from *Gay Divorcee*)

Words and Music by Cole Porter
Arranged by Dan Coates

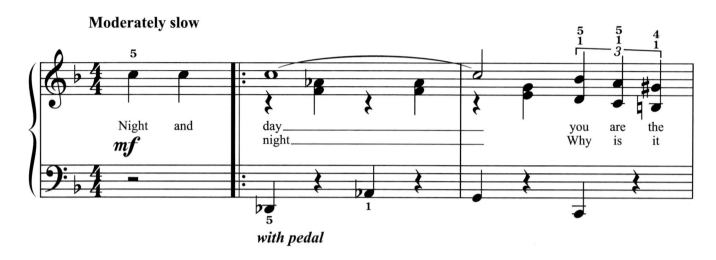

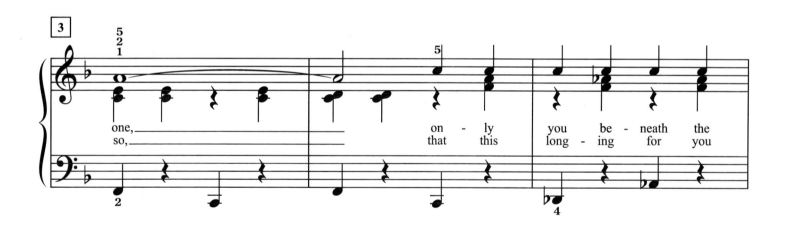

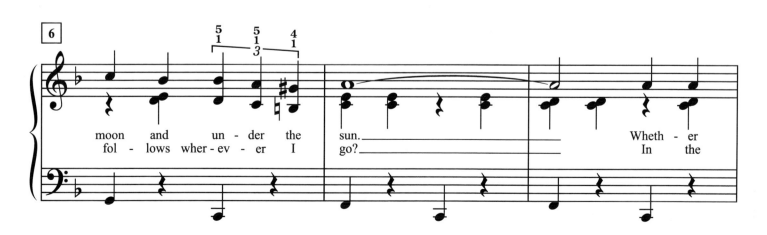

near to me or far, it's no mat - ter, dar - ling,
roar - ing traf - fic's boom, in the si - lence of my

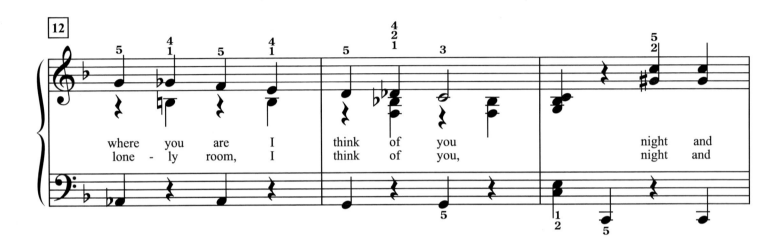

where you are I think of you night and
lone - ly room, I think of you, you, night and

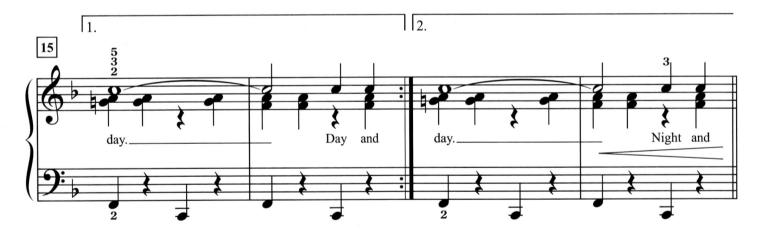

day. Day and
day. Night and

day un - der the hide of me,

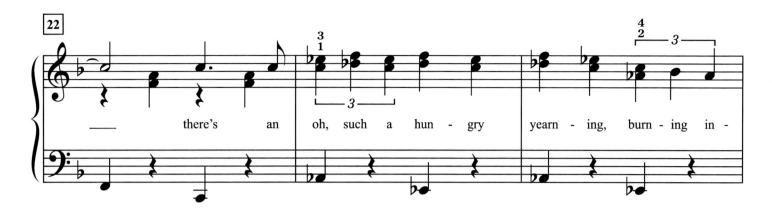

there's an oh, such a hun - gry yearn - ing, burn - ing in -

side of me. And its tor - ment won't be

through 'til you let me spend my life mak - ing love to you,

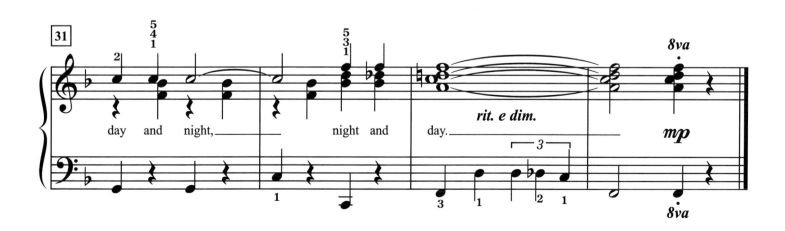

day and night, night and day.

NEED YOU NOW

Words and Music by
Dave Haywood, Charles Kelley,
Hillary Scott and Josh Kear
Arranged by Dan Coates

Moderately

Verse:

1. Pic - ture per - fect mem - 'ries,   scat - tered all a - round   the floor.
2. *See additional lyrics.*

with pedal

Reach-ing for the phone, 'cause   I can't fight it an - y - more.

And I won - der - if___ I ev - er cross___ your mind.___   For me it hap -

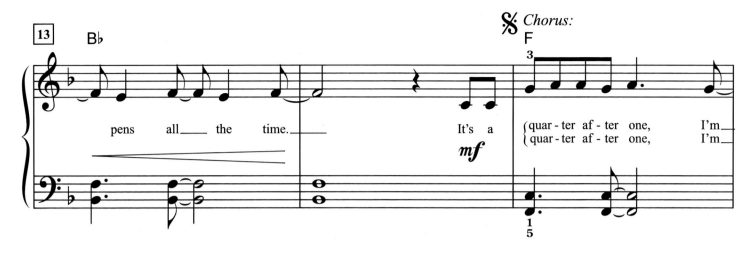

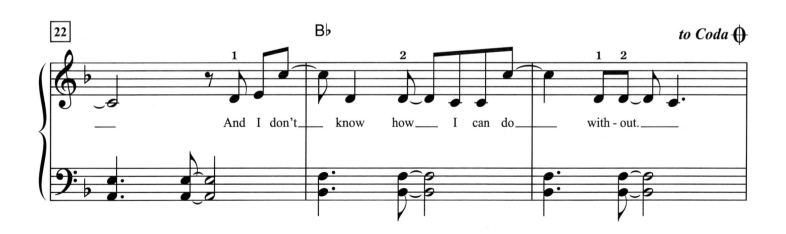

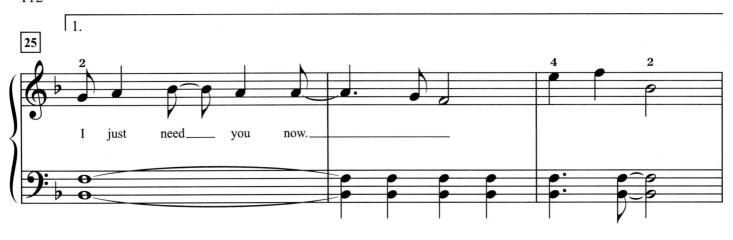

I just need___ you now.___

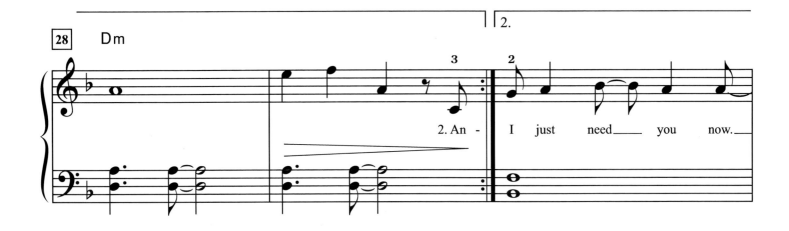

2. An - I just need___ you now.___

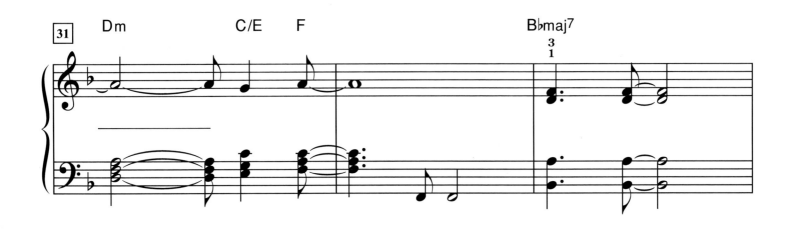

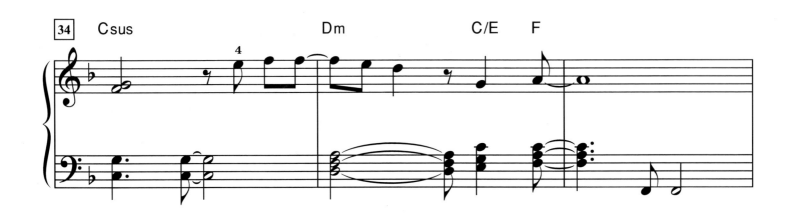

Verse 2:
Another shot of whiskey, can't stop looking at the door,
Wishing you'd come sweeping in the way you did before.
And I wonder if I ever cross your mind.
For me it happens all the time.
(To Chorus:)

NOT LIKE THE MOVIES

Words and Music by
Katy Perry and Greg Wells
Arranged by Dan Coates

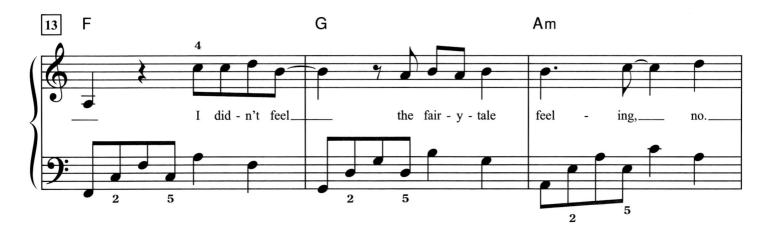

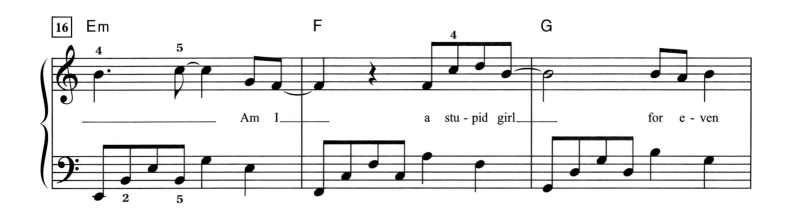

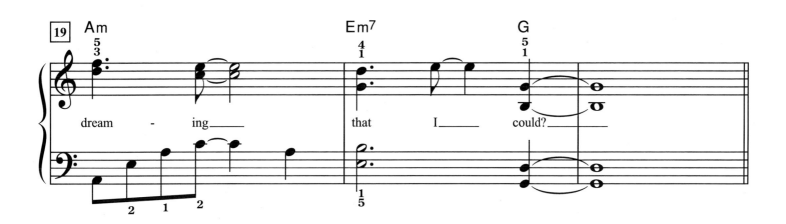

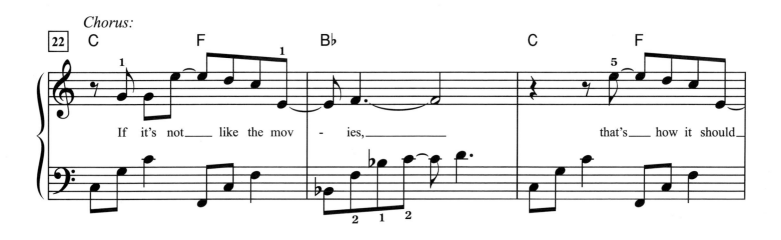

When he's the one, I'll come un - done, and my world will stop

spin - ning._____ And that's just the be - gin - ing,_____

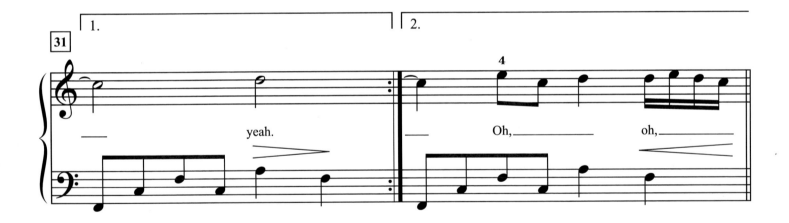

_____ yeah. _____ Oh,_____ oh,_____

Bridge:

yeah. 'Cause I know__ you're out there. And you're,___ you're look - ing__ for

mf

Verse 2:
Snow White said when I was young,
"One day my prince will come."
So I wait for that date.
They say it's hard to meet your match,
Gotta find my better half,
So we make perfect shapes.
If stars don't align, if it doesn't stop time,
If you can't see the sign, wait for it.
One hundred percent, worth every penny spent,
He'll be the one that finishes your sentences.
(To Chorus:)

THE NOTEBOOK

Written by Aaron Zigman
Arranged by Dan Coates

OPEN ARMS

Words and Music by
Jonathan Cain and Steve Perry
Arranged by Dan Coates

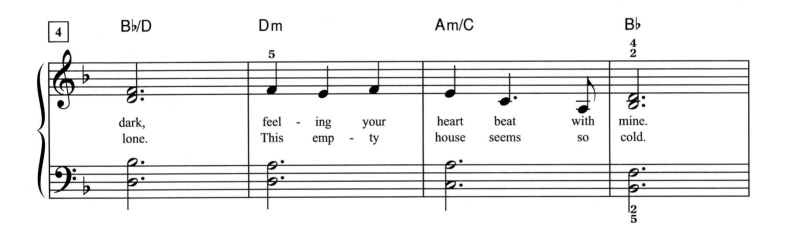

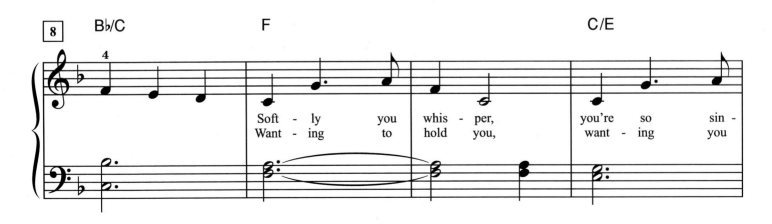

123

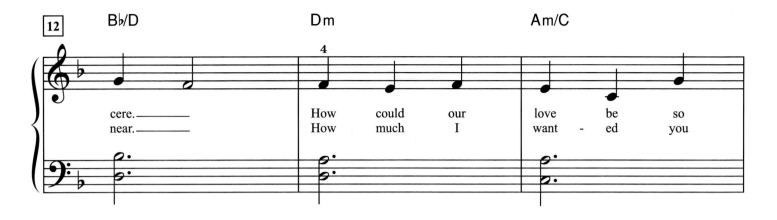

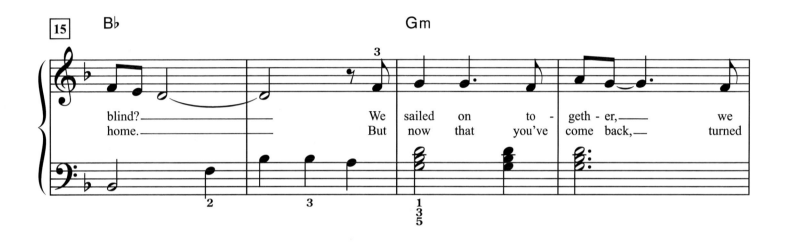

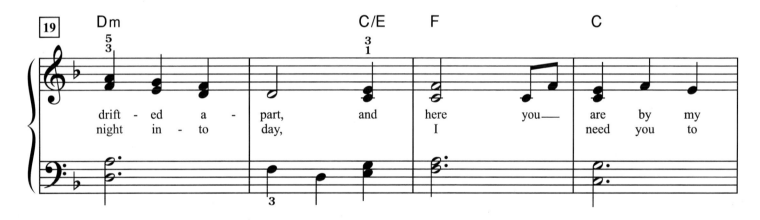

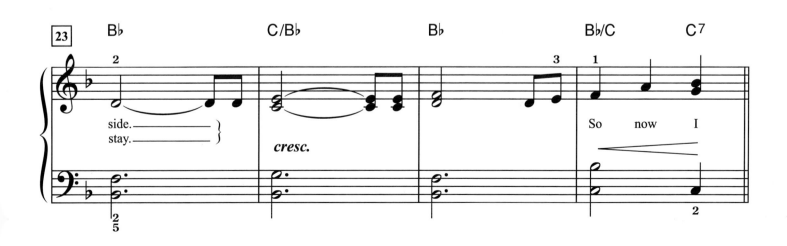

Chorus:

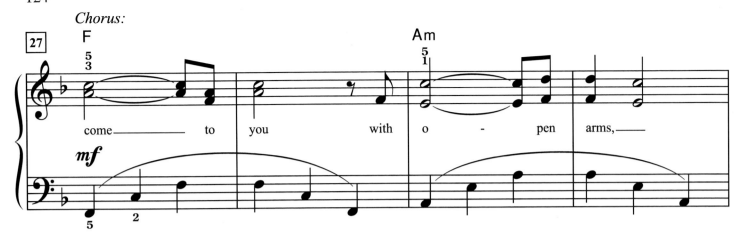

come _____ to you with o - pen arms, ——

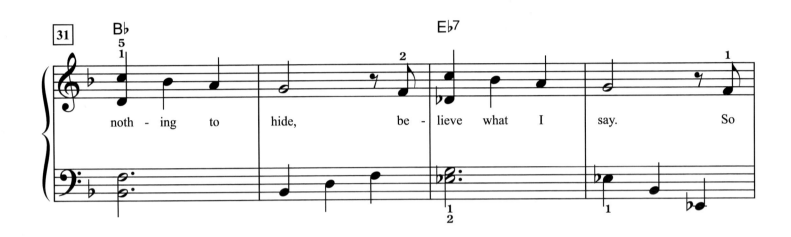

noth - ing to hide, be - lieve what I say. So

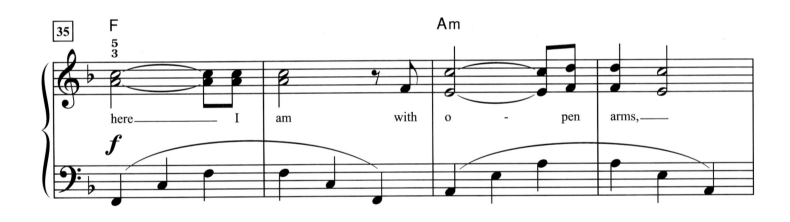

here _____ I am with o - pen arms, ——

hop - ing to see what your love means to

THE ONLY EXCEPTION

Words and Music by
Hayley Williams and Josh Farro
Arranged by Dan Coates

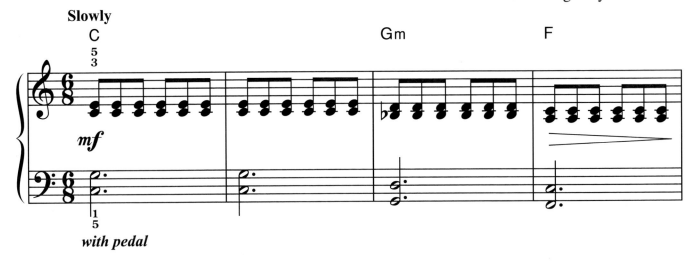

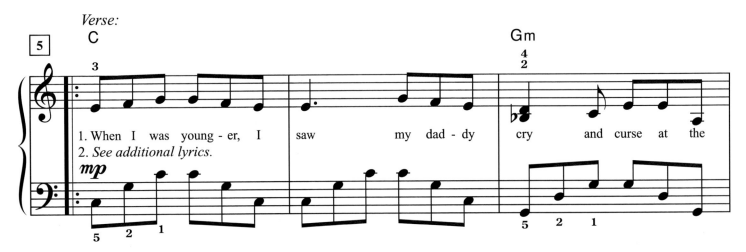

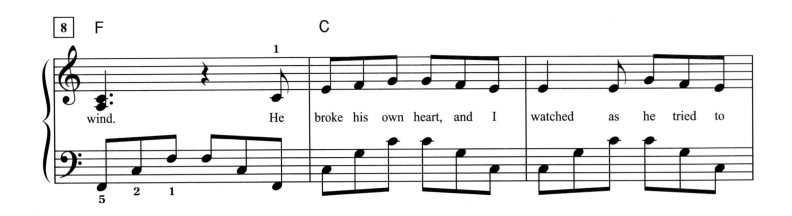

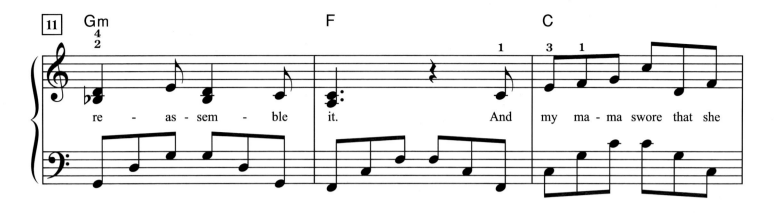

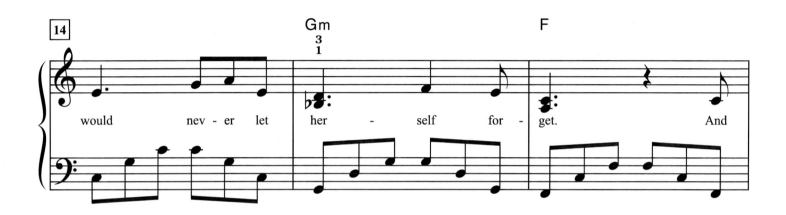

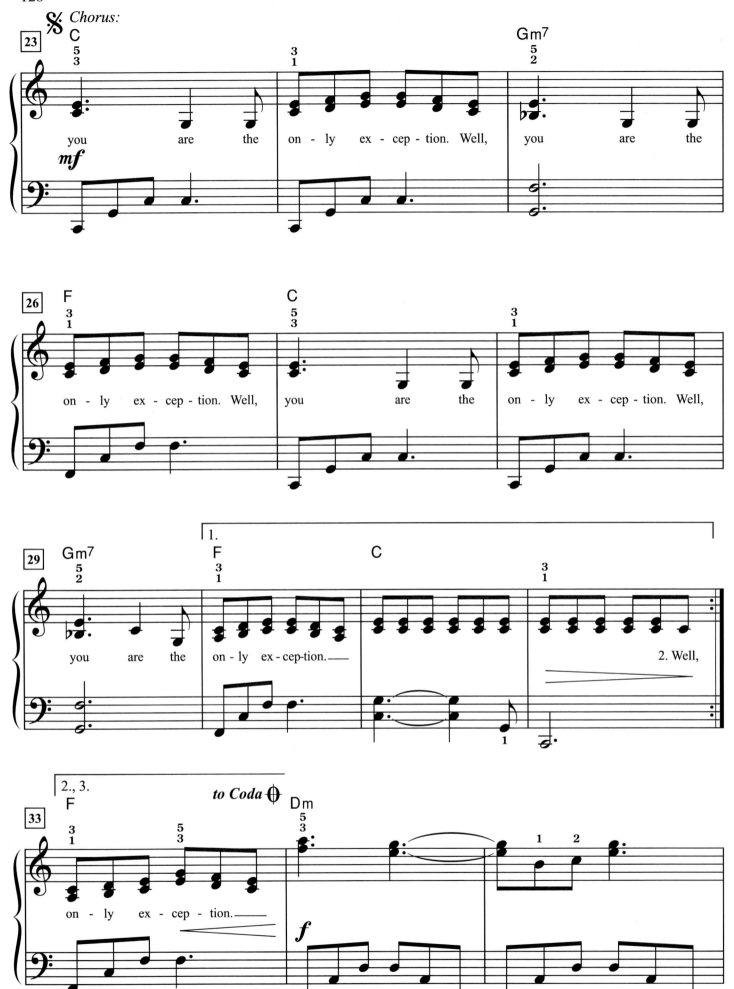

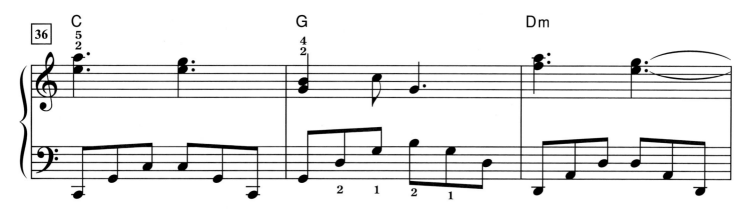

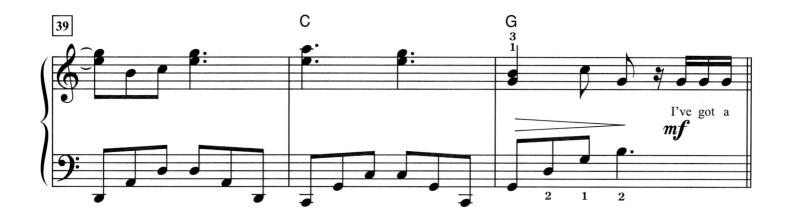

Bridge:

tight grip on re - al - i - ty, but I can't_____ let go of what's in front of me_____

here._____ I know you're leav - ing in the morn - ing when you wake up. Leave me

Verse 2:
Well, maybe I know somewhere
Deep in my soul
That love never lasts.
And we've got to find other ways
To make it alone,
Or keep a straight face.
And I've always lived like this,
Keeping a comfortable distance.
And up until now I had sworn to myself
That I'm content with loneliness,
Because none of it was ever worth the risk.
(To Chorus:)

OUT HERE ON MY OWN

(from *Fame*)

Music by Michael Gore
Lyrics by Lesley Gore
Arranged by Dan Coates

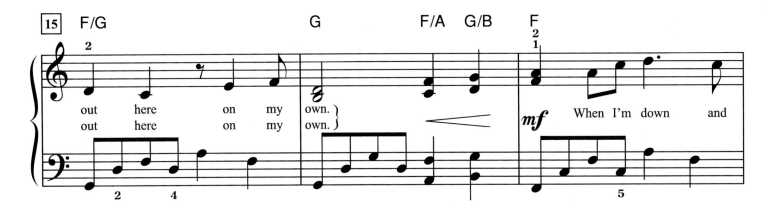

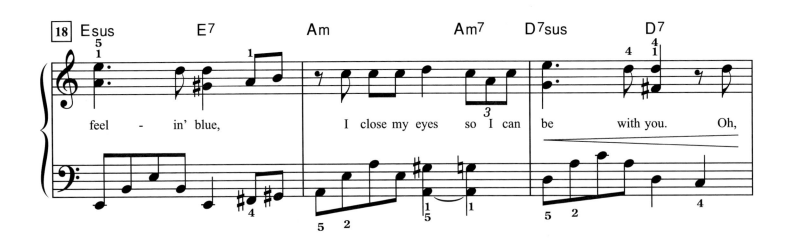

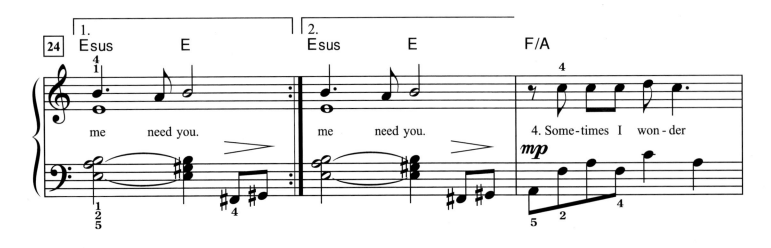

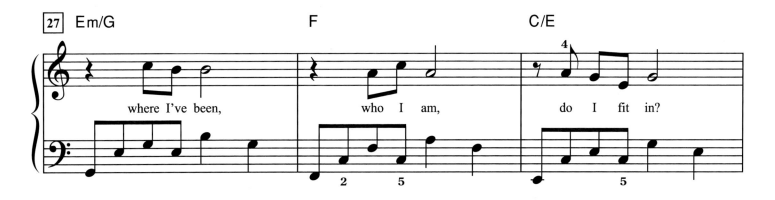

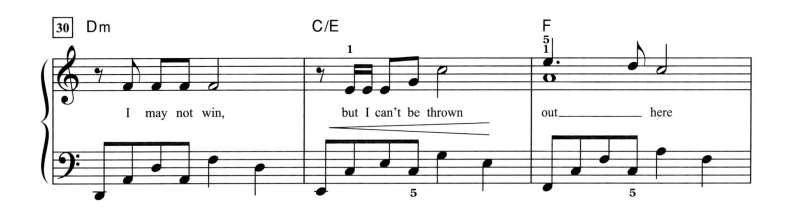

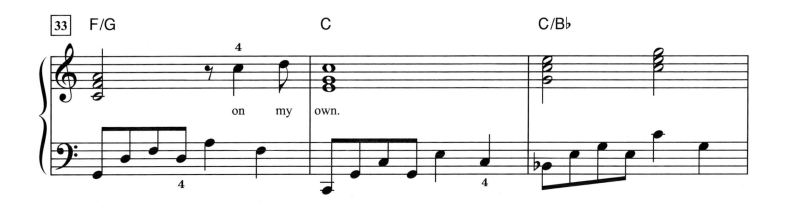

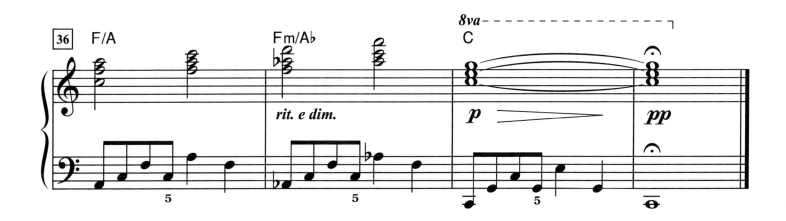

PEOPLE

(from *Funny Girl*)

Words by Bob Merrill
Music by Jule Styne
Arranged by Dan Coates

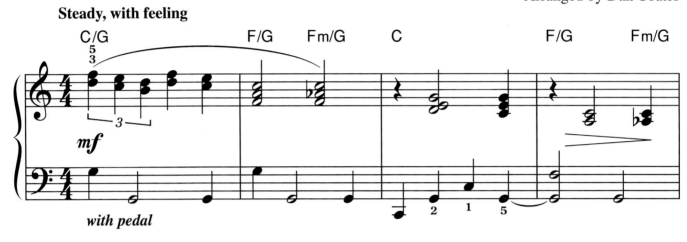

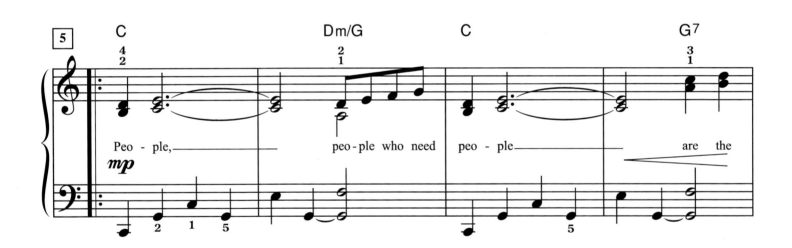

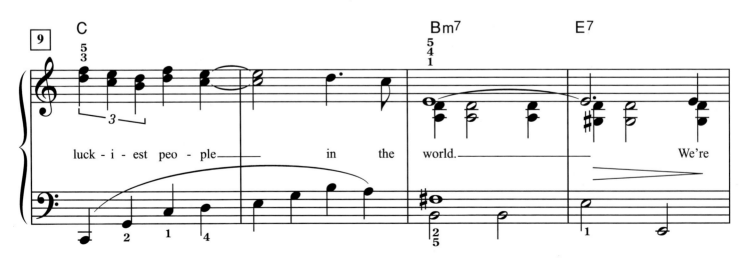

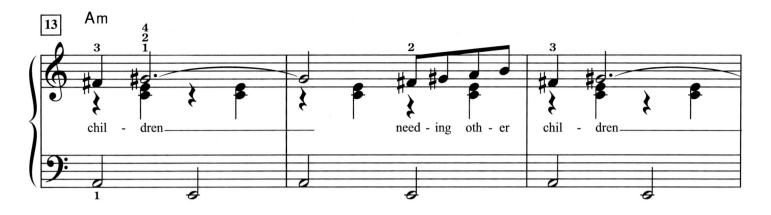

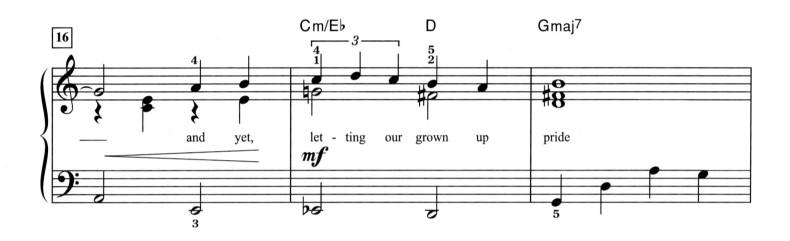

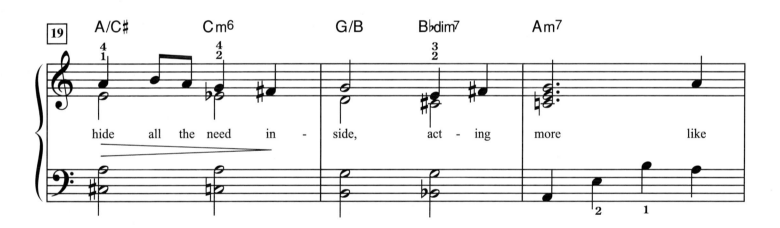

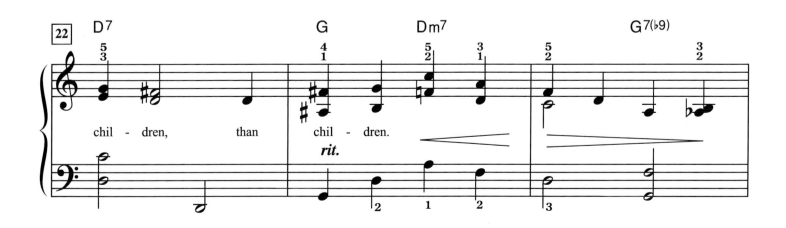

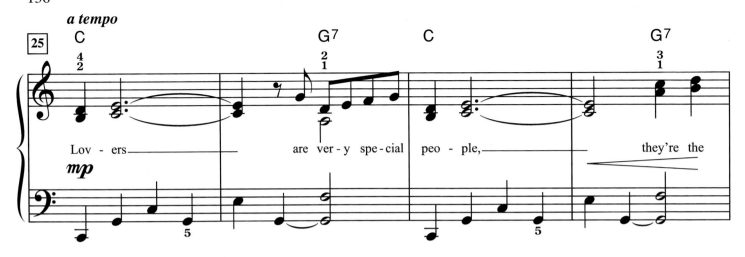

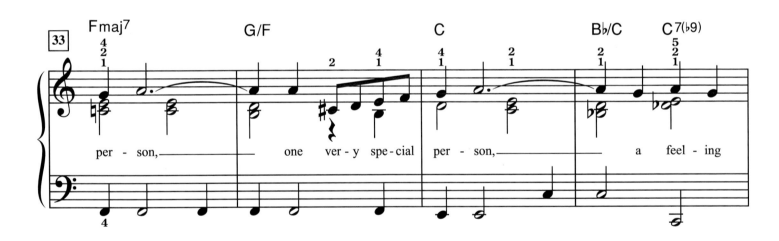

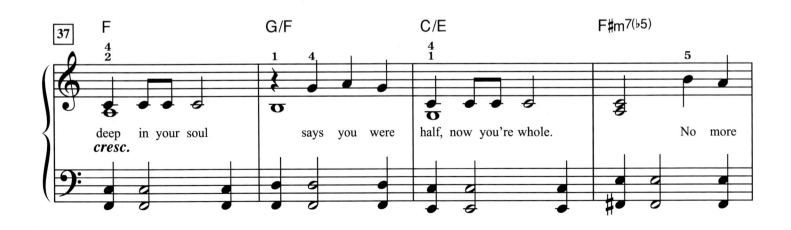

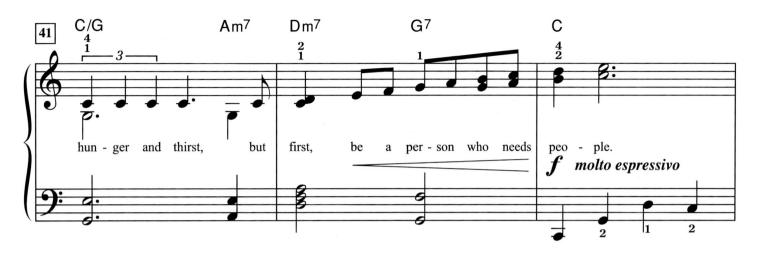

hun - ger and thirst, but first, be a per - son who needs peo - ple.

f molto espressivo

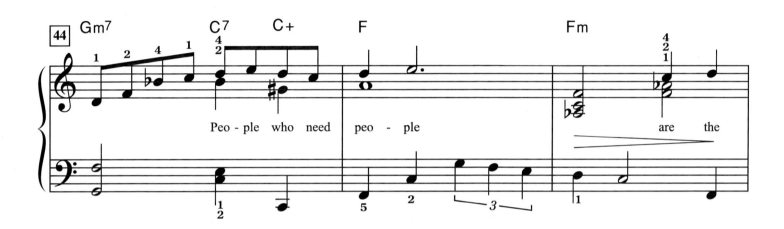

Peo - ple who need peo - ple are the

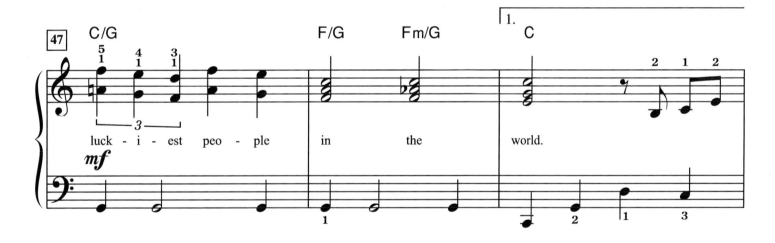

luck - i - est peo - ple in the world.

mf

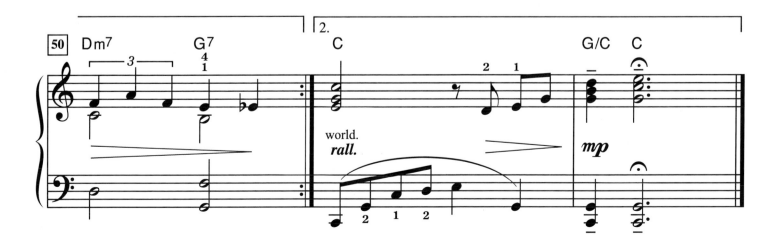

world.
rall.

mp

SKYLARK

Words by Johnny Mercer
Music by Hoagy Carmichael
Arranged by Dan Coates

Slowly, with expression

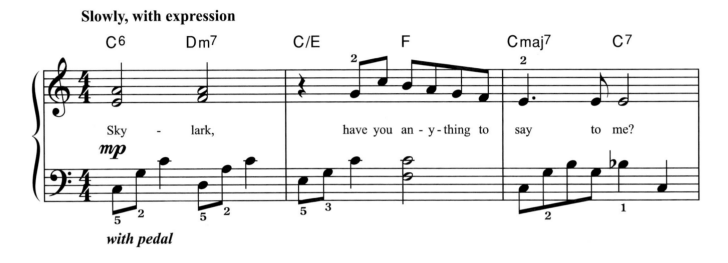

Sky - lark, have you an - y - thing to say to me?

Won't you tell me where my love can be? Is there a mea - dow in the

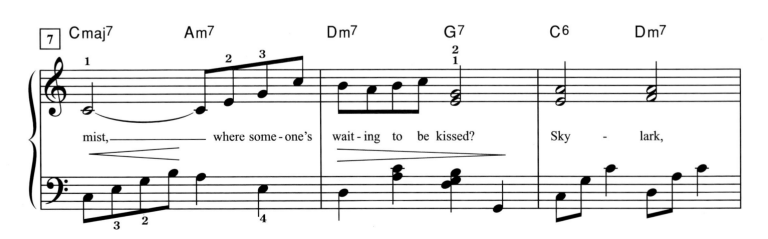

mist,_____ where some - one's wait - ing to be kissed? Sky - lark,

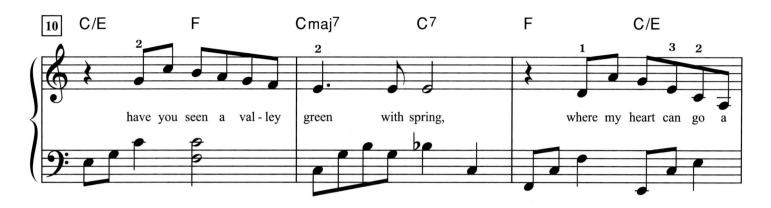

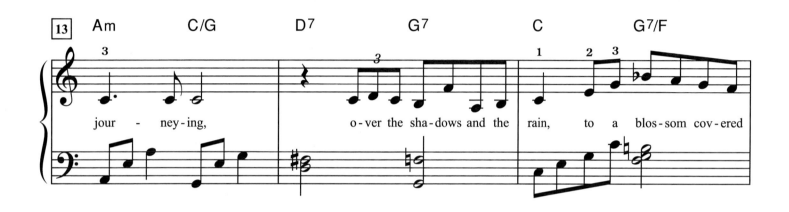

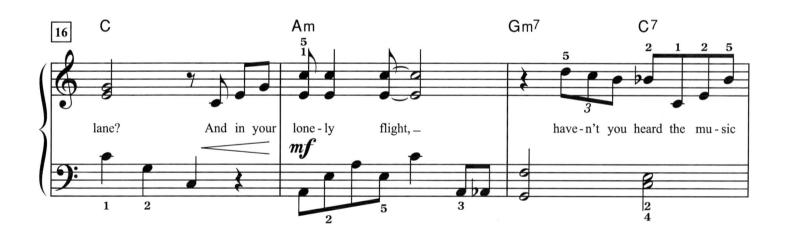

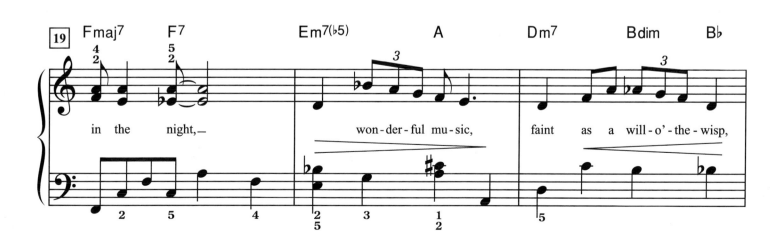

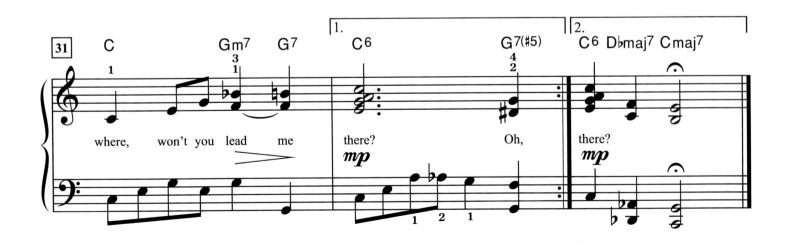

SO IN LOVE

(from *Kiss Me Kate*)

Words and Music by Cole Porter
Arranged by Dan Coates

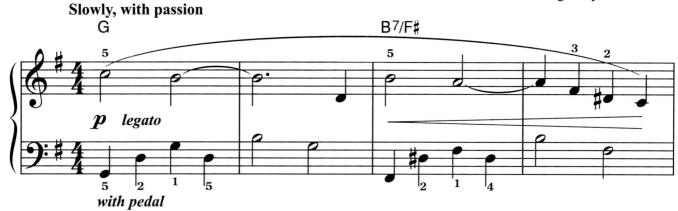

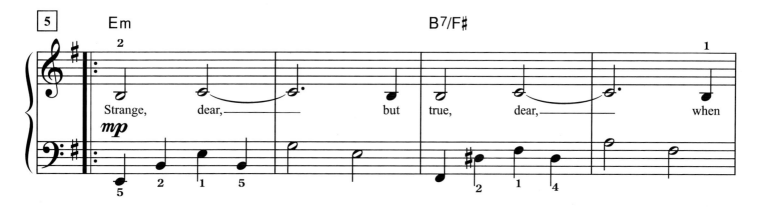

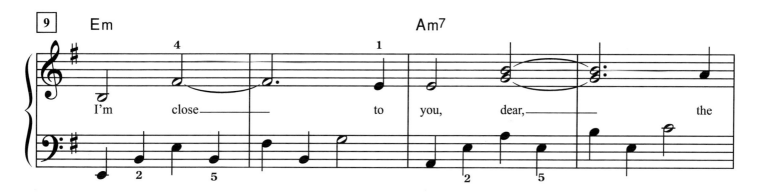

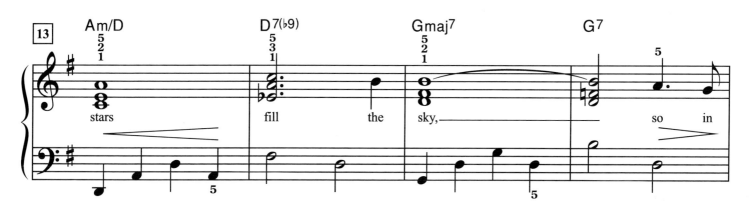

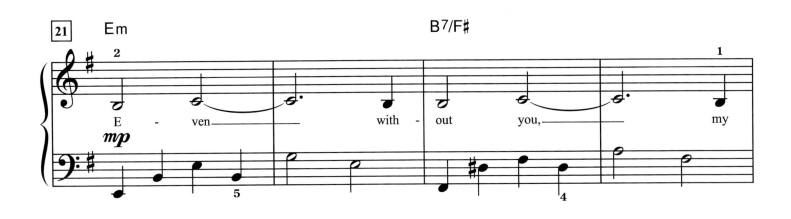

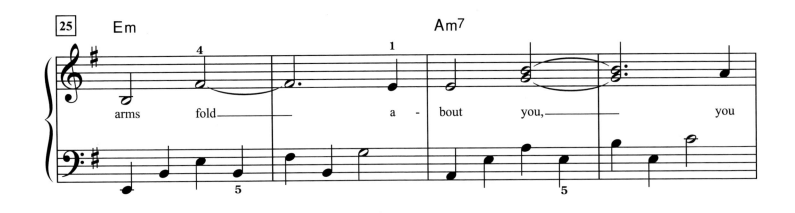

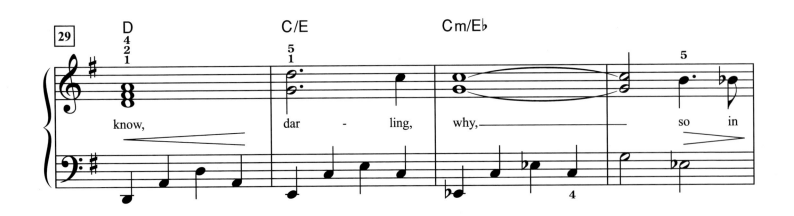

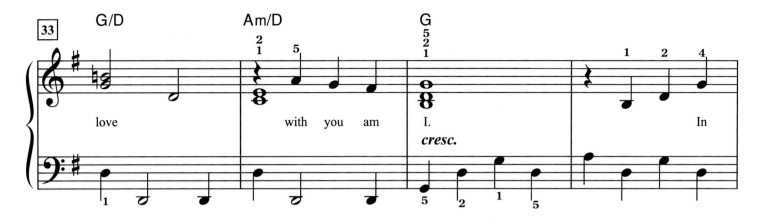

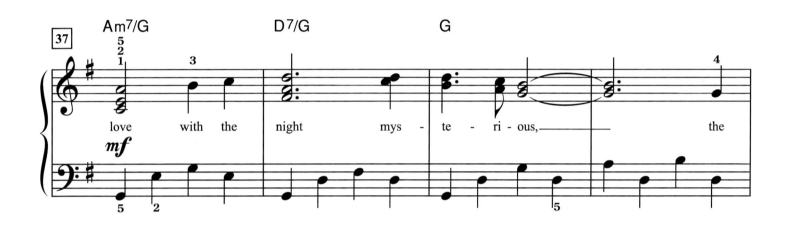

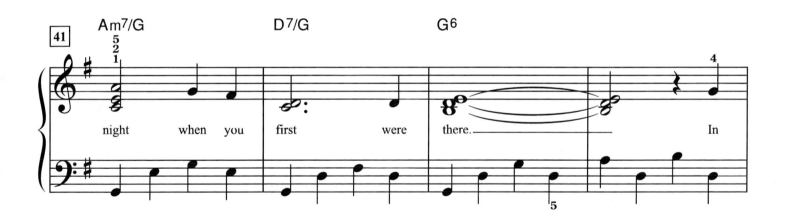

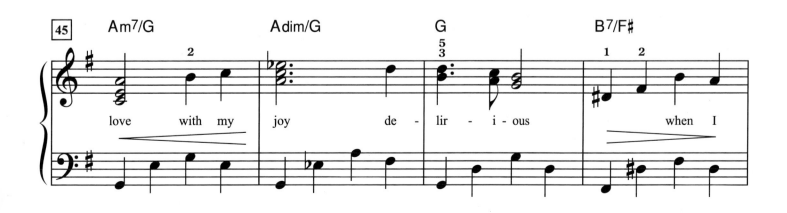

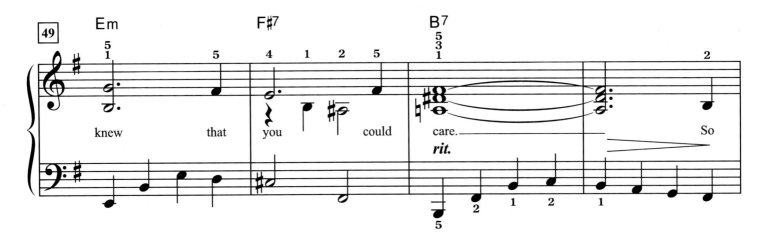

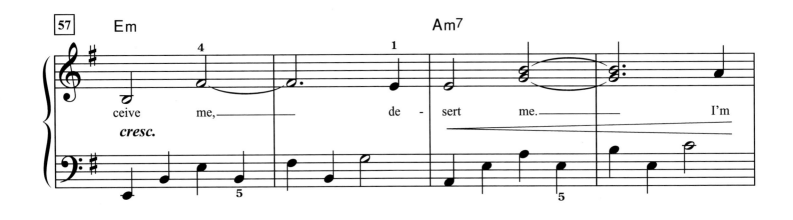

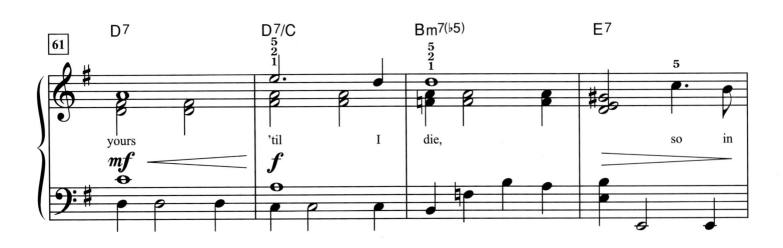

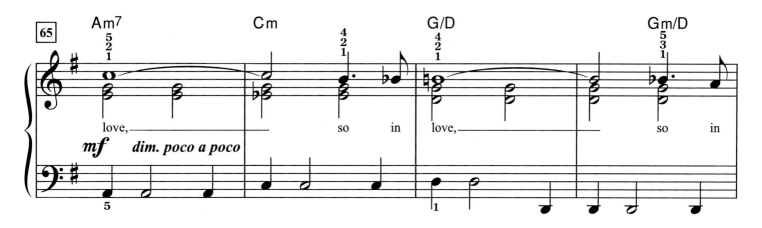

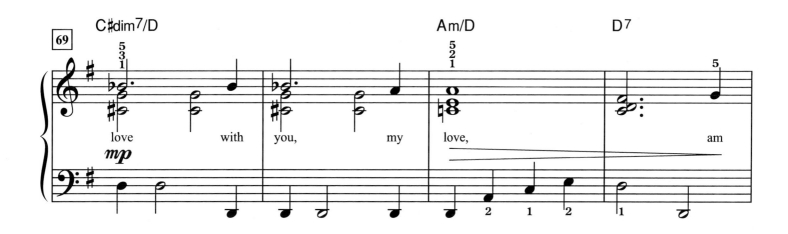

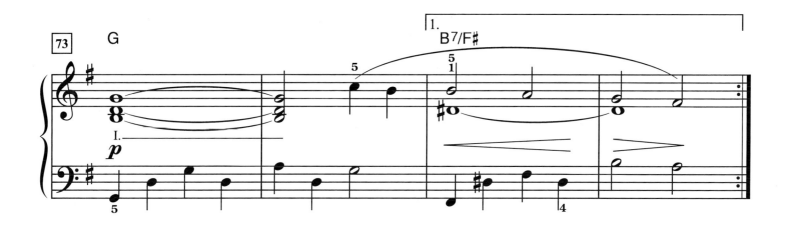

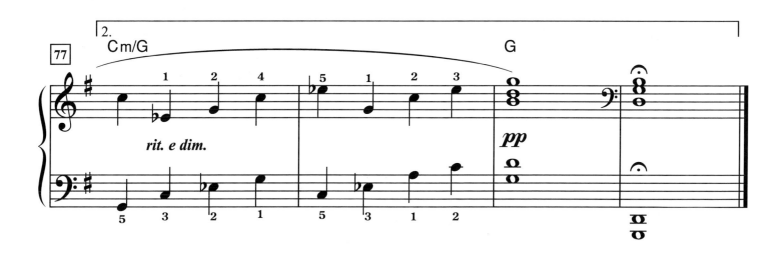

STAR DUST

Music by Hoagy Carmichael
Words by Mitchell Parish
French Translation by Yvette Baruch
Arranged by Dan Coates

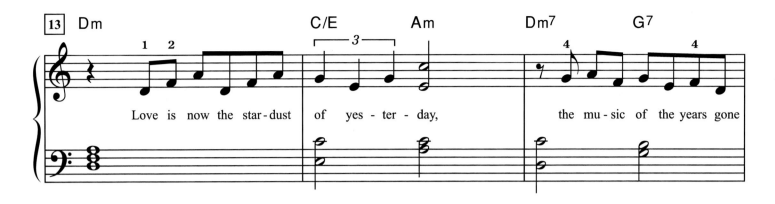

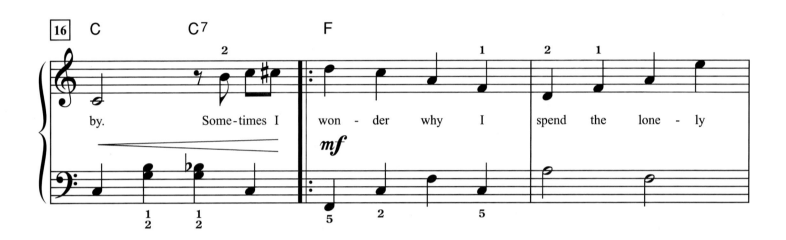

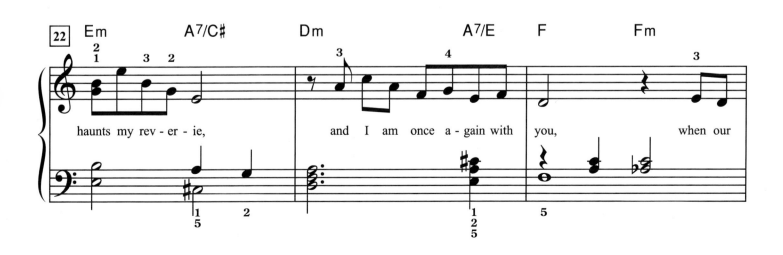

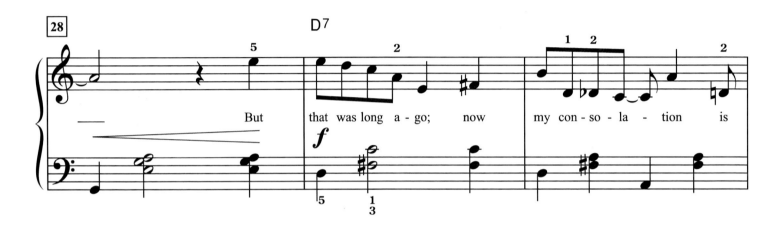

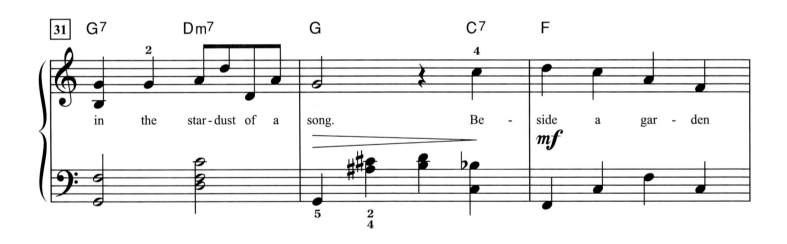

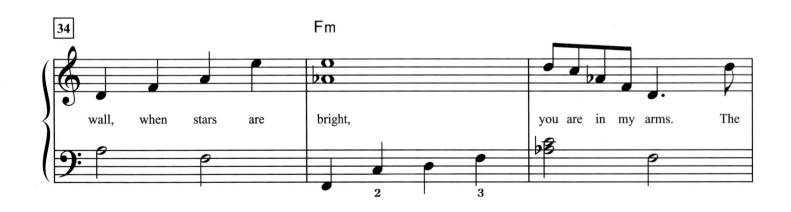

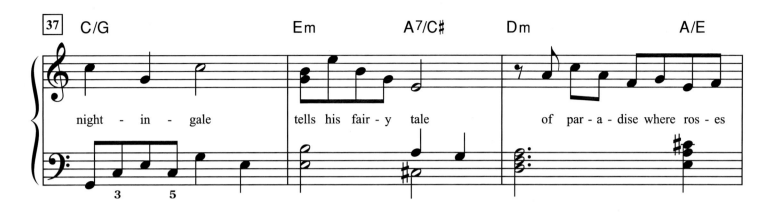

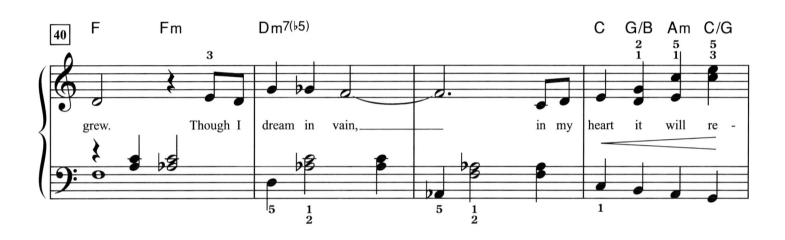

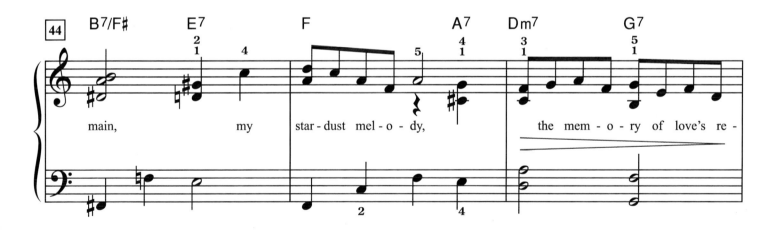

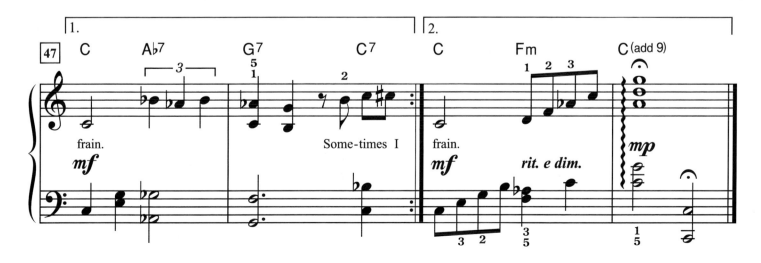

SOMEONE TO WATCH OVER ME

(from *Oh, Kay!*)

Music and Lyrics by
George Gershwin and Ira Gershwin
Arranged by Dan Coates

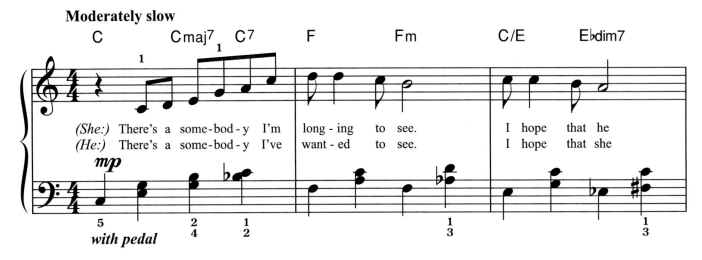

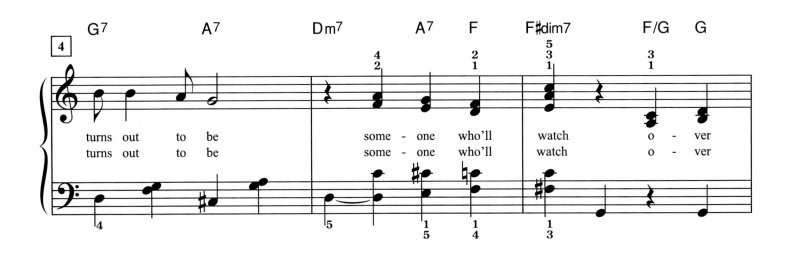

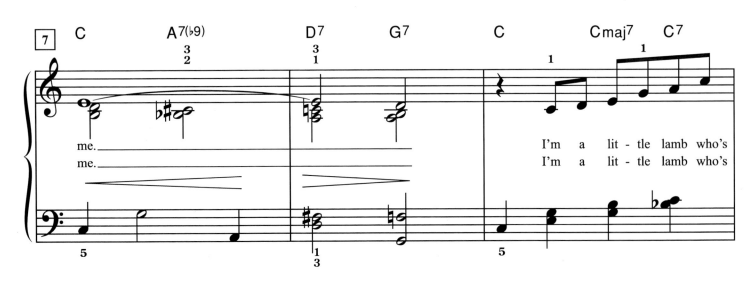

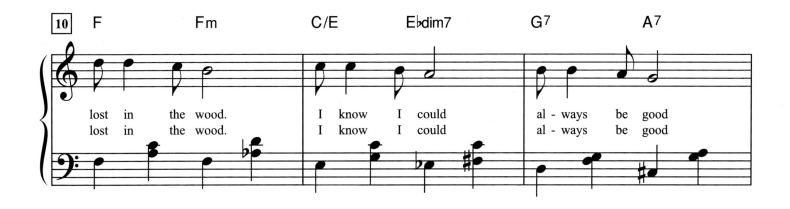

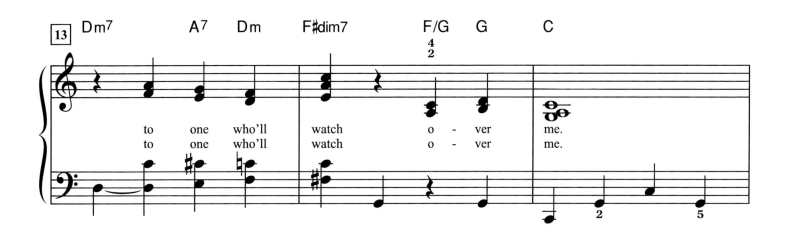

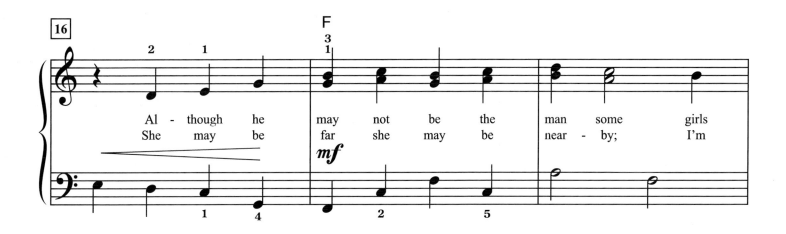

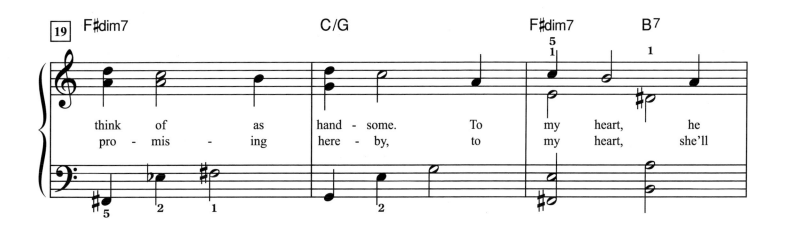

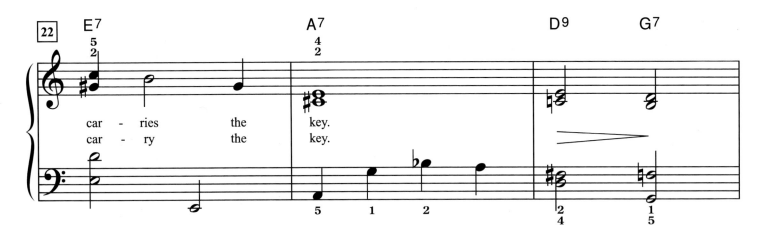

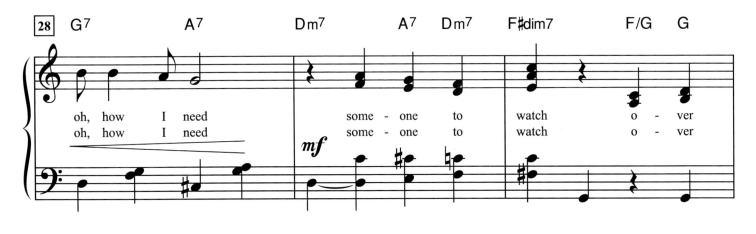

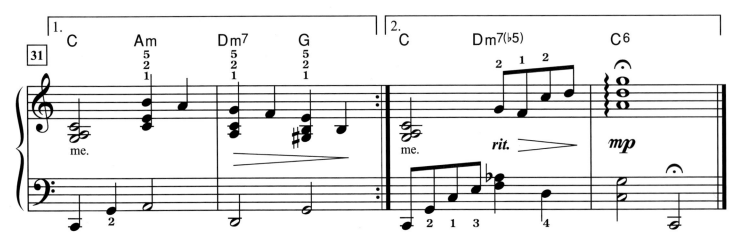

THANK YOU

Words and Music by
Dido Armstrong and Paul Herman
Arranged by Dan Coates

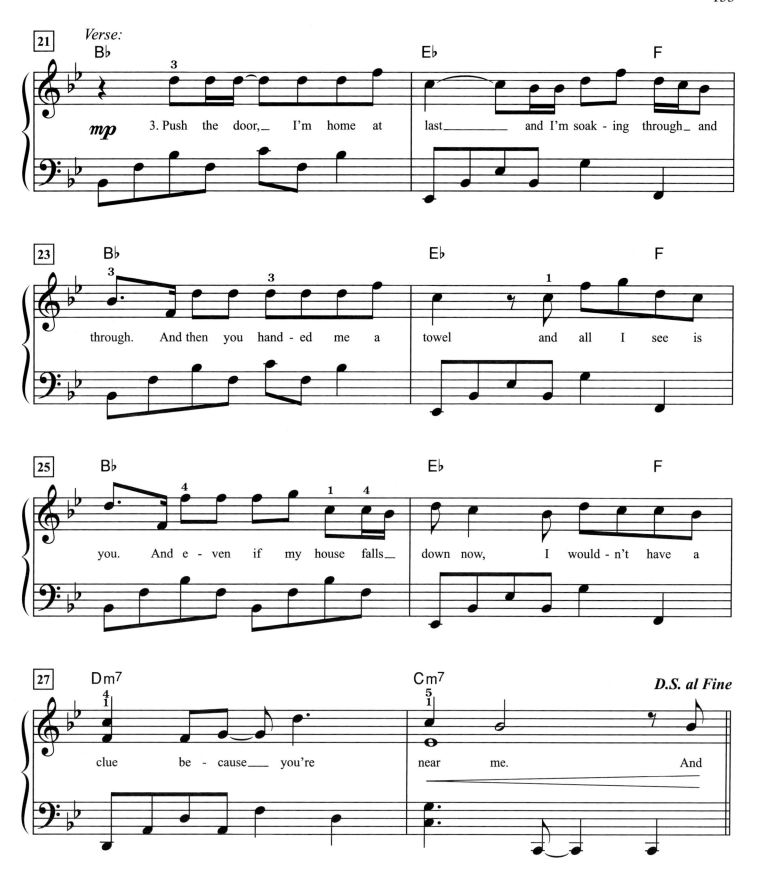

Verse 2:
I drank too much last night, got bills to pay,
My head just feels in pain.
I missed the bus and there'll be hell today,
I'm late for work again.
And even if I'm there, they'll all imply
That I might not last the day.
And then you call me and it's not so bad, it's not so bad.
(To Chorus:)

TAKE MY BREATH AWAY

Music by Giorgio Moroder
Words by Tom Whitlock
Arranged by Dan Coates

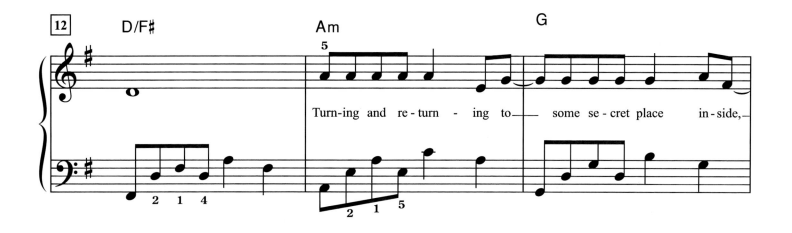

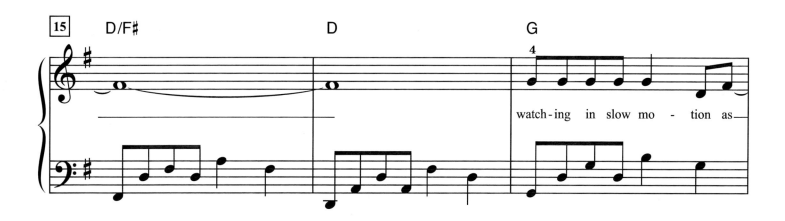

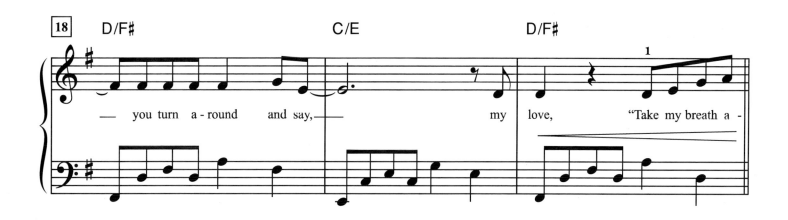

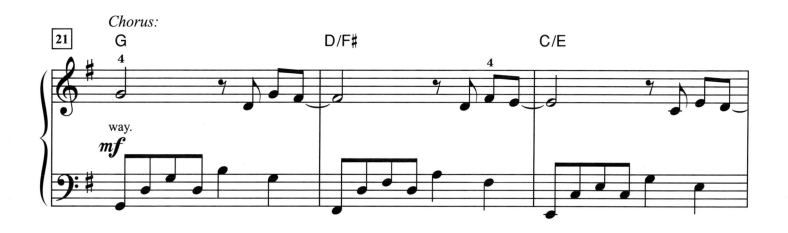

TO WHERE YOU ARE

Words and Music by
Richard Marx and Linda Thompson
Arranged by Dan Coates

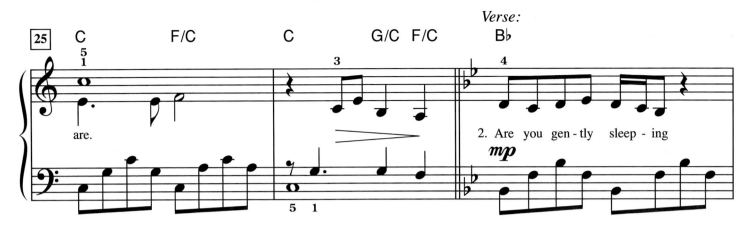

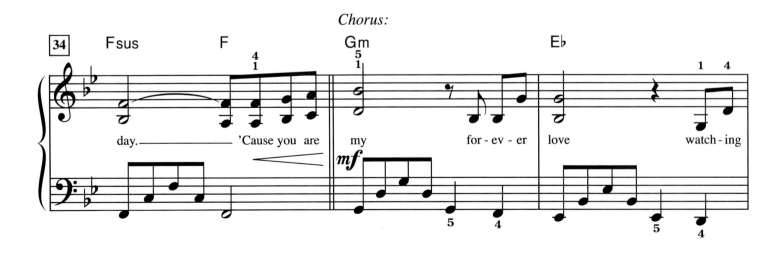

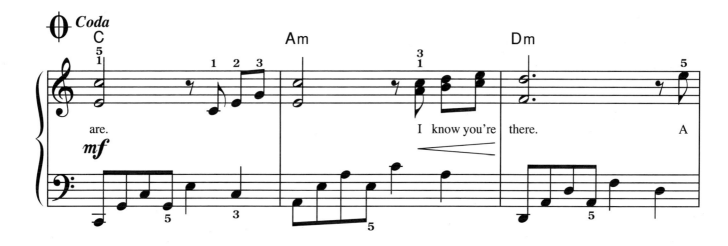

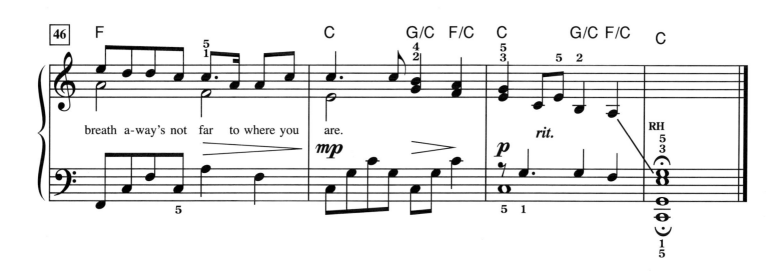

UNBREAK MY HEART

Words and Music by Diane Warren
Arranged by Dan Coates

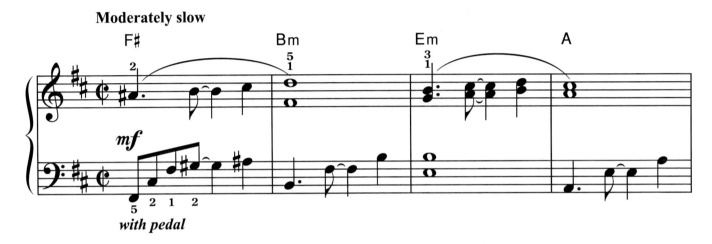

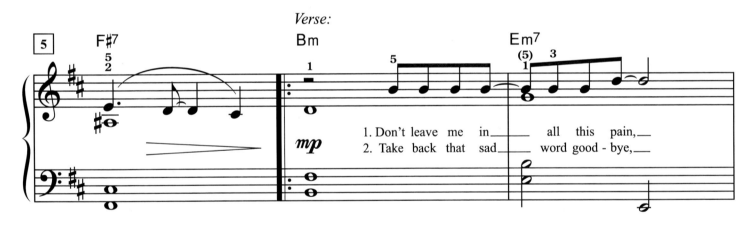

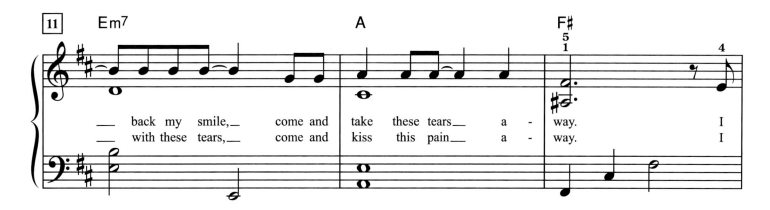

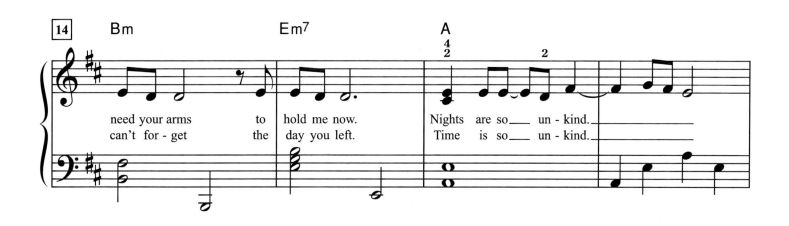

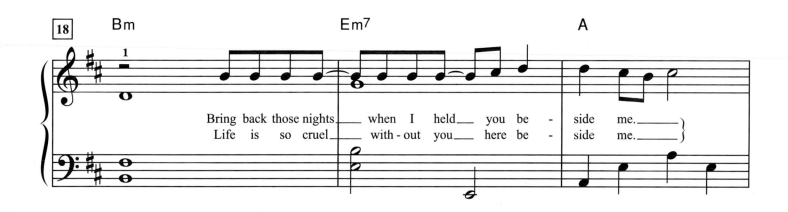

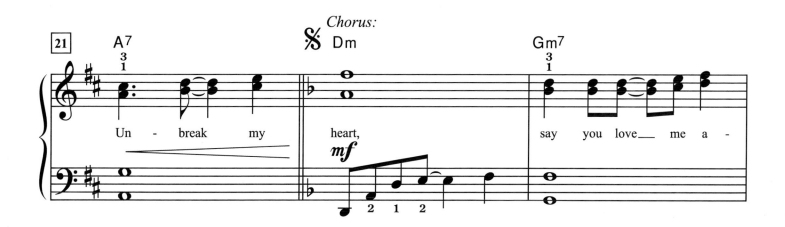

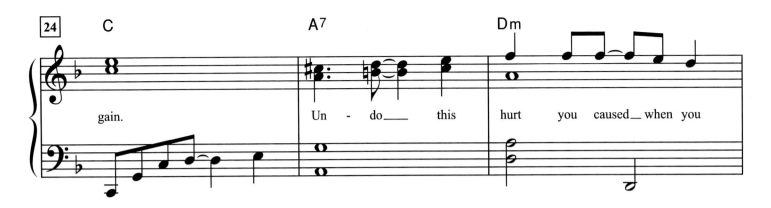

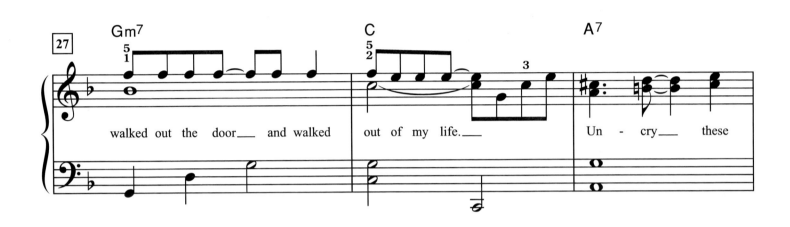

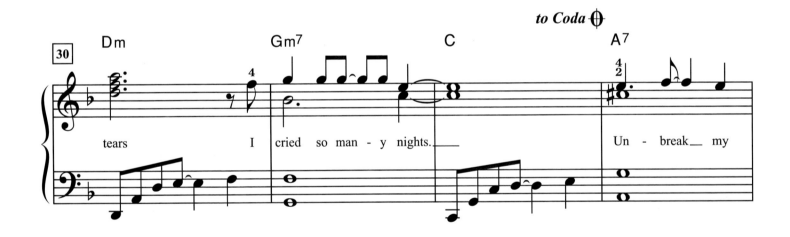

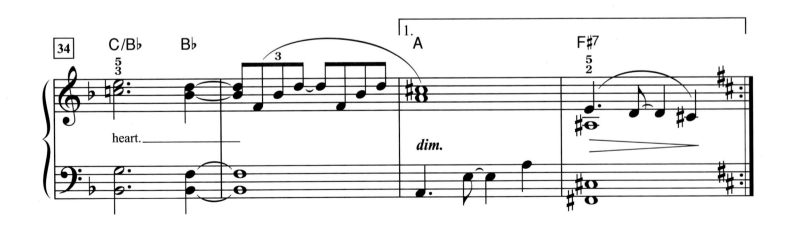

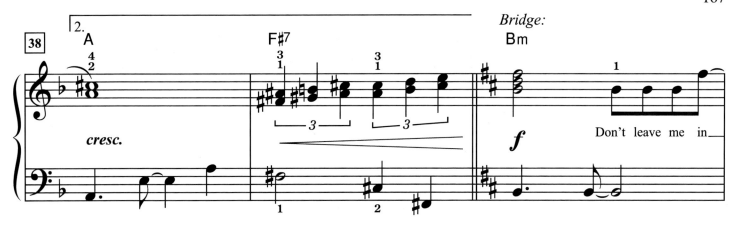

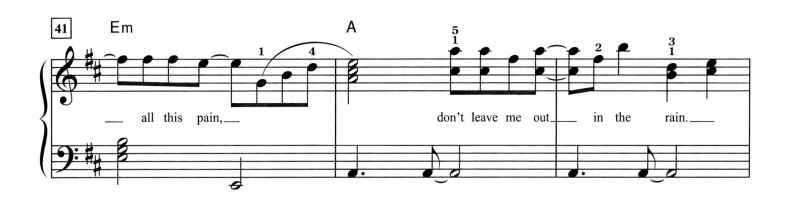

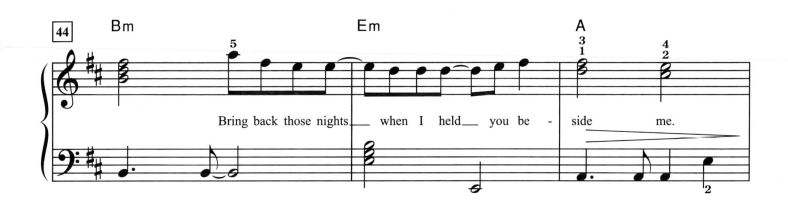

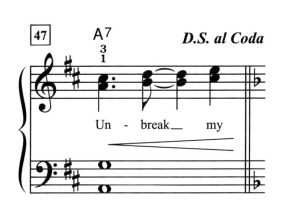

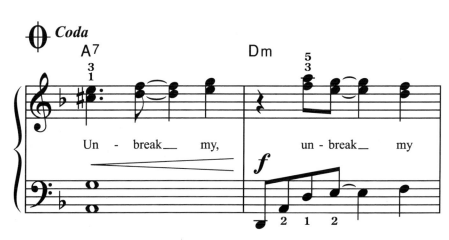

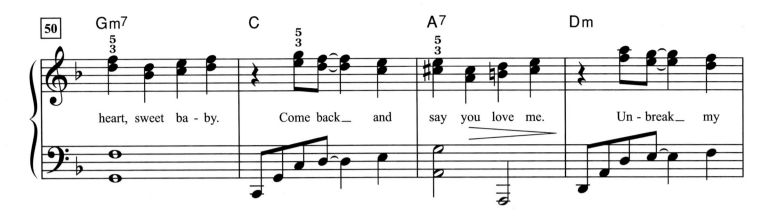

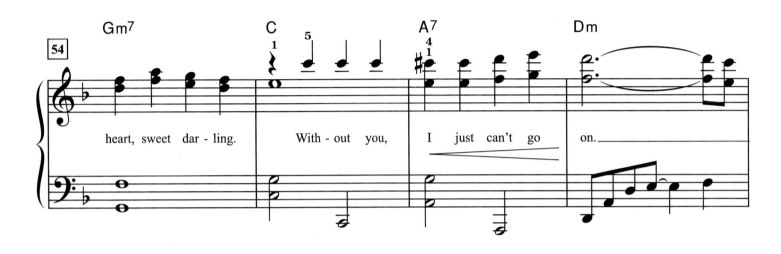

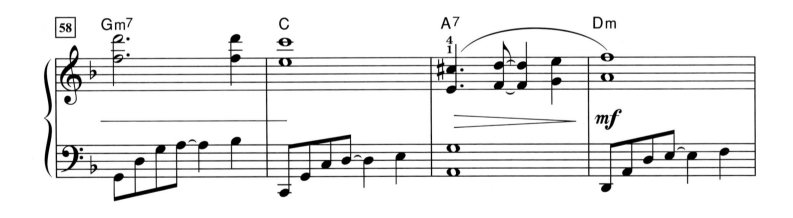

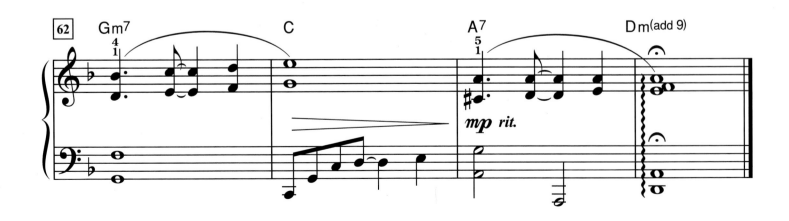

WHO'S SORRY NOW

Music by Ted Snyder
Words by Bert Kalmar and Harry Ruby
Arranged by Dan Coates

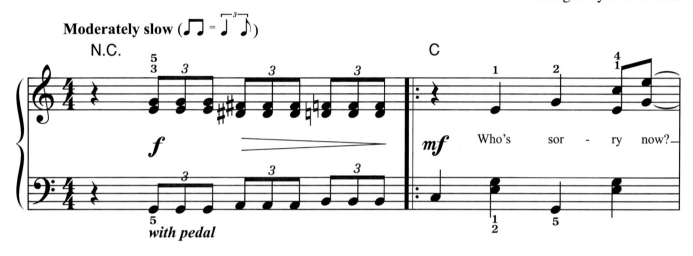

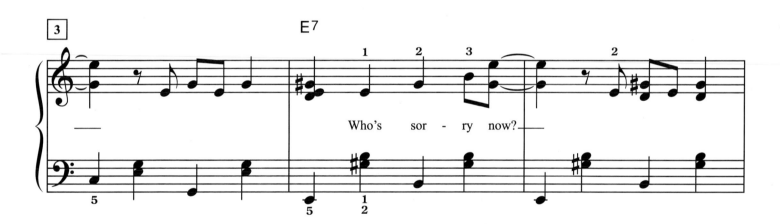

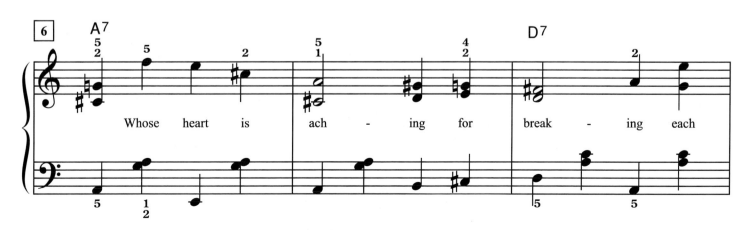

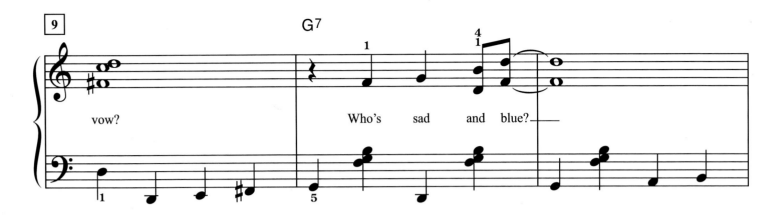

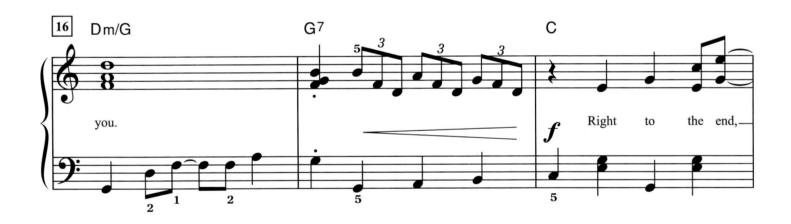

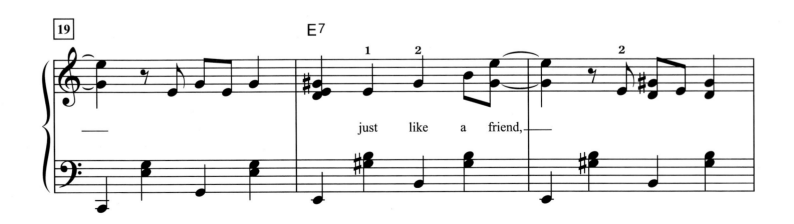

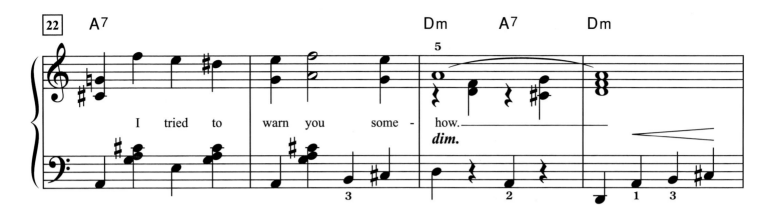

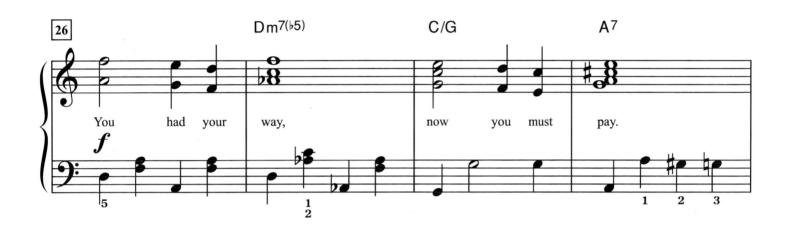

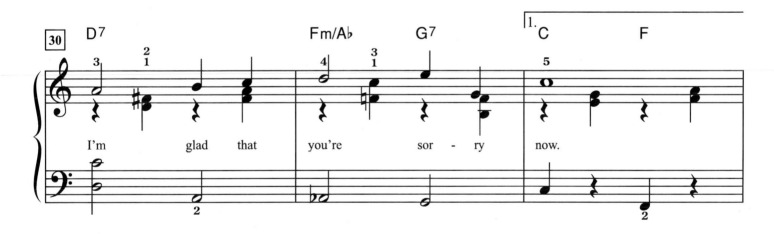

WAY BACK INTO LOVE

(from *Music and Lyrics*)

Words and Music by Adam Schlesinger
Arranged by Dan Coates

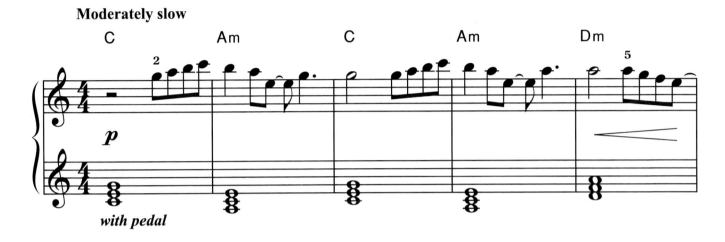

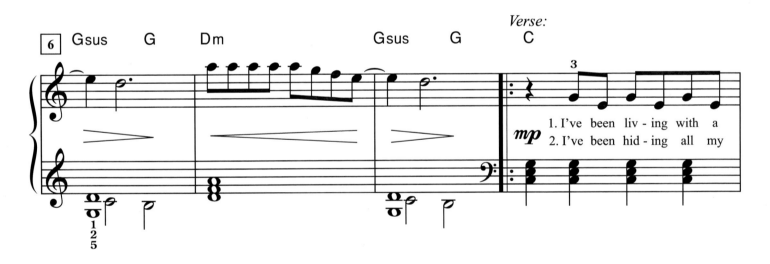

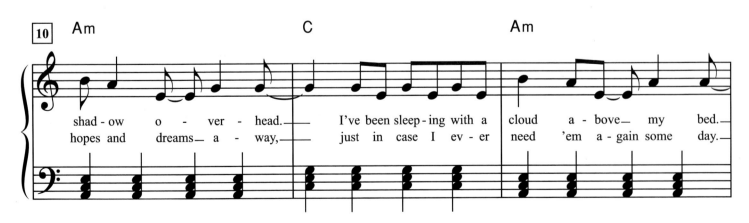

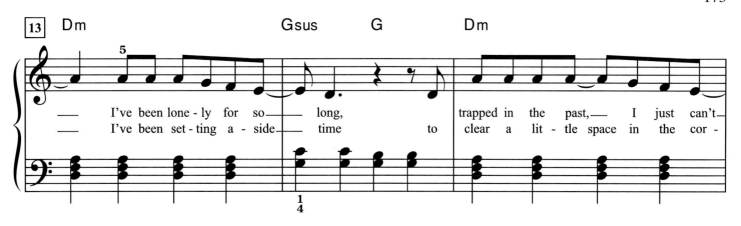

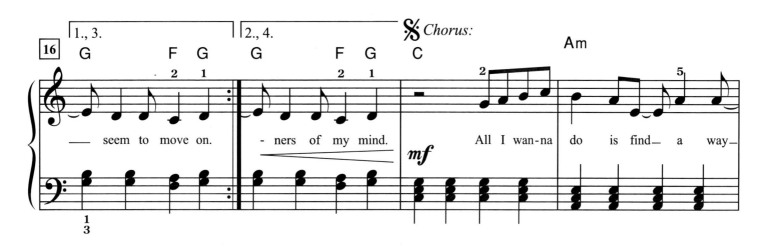

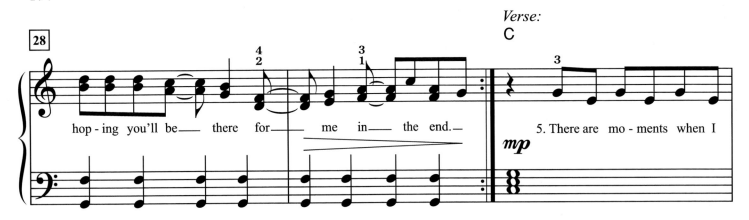

Verse:
C

28 hop-ing you'll be there for me in the end.

5. There are mo-ments when I

31 Am · C · Am

don't know if it's real, or if an-y-bod-y feels the way I feel.

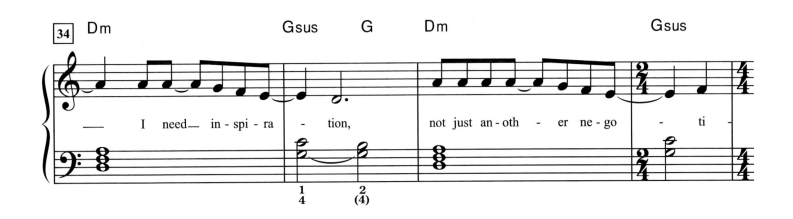

34 Dm · Gsus G · Dm · Gsus

I need in-spi-ra - tion, not just an-oth - er ne-go - ti -

D.S. al Coda

Coda
Am

38 G

a - tion.

you'll show me what to do.

And if you

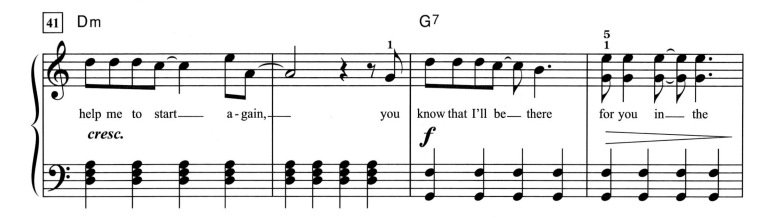

help me to start— a - gain,— you know that I'll be— there for you in— the

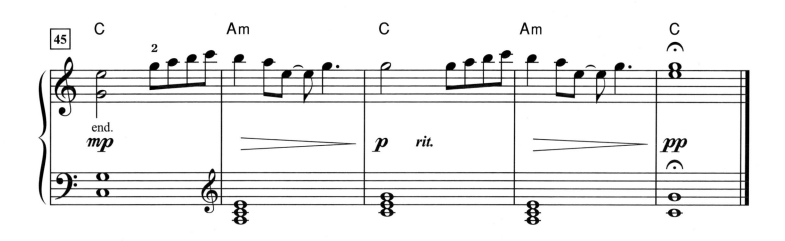

Verse 3:
I've been watching, but the stars refuse to shine.
I've been searching, but I just don't see the signs.
I know that it's out there.
There's got to be something for my soul, somewhere.

Verse 4:
I've been looking for someone to shed some light,
Not somebody just to get me through the night.
I could use some direction,
And I'm open to your suggestions.
(To Chorus:)

WEEKEND IN NEW ENGLAND

Words and Music by Randy Edelman
Arranged by Dan Coates

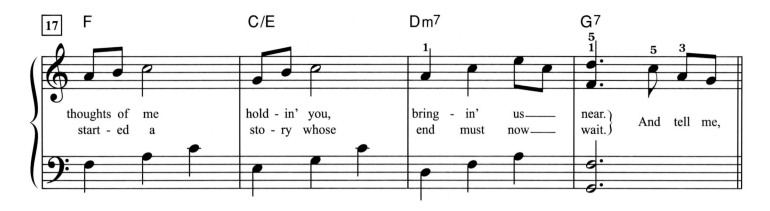

17 F   C/E   Dm7   G7

thoughts of me   hold - in' you,   bring - in' us —— near.⎫ And tell me,
start - ed a   sto - ry whose   end must now —— wait.⎭

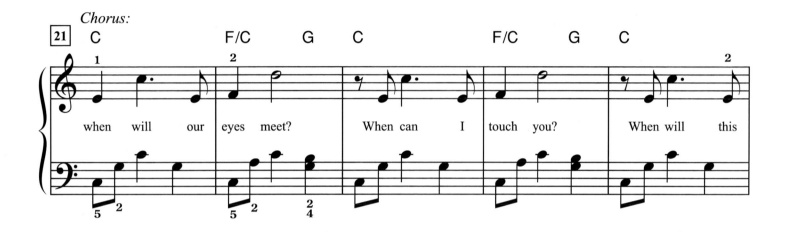

Chorus:

21 C   F/C   G   C   F/C   G   C

when will our eyes meet?   When can I touch you?   When will this

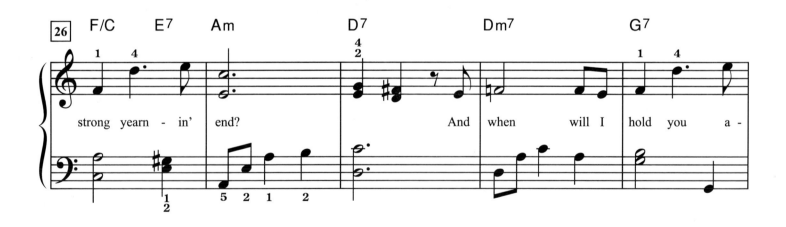

26 F/C   E7   Am   D7   Dm7   G7

strong yearn - in' end?   And when will I hold you a -

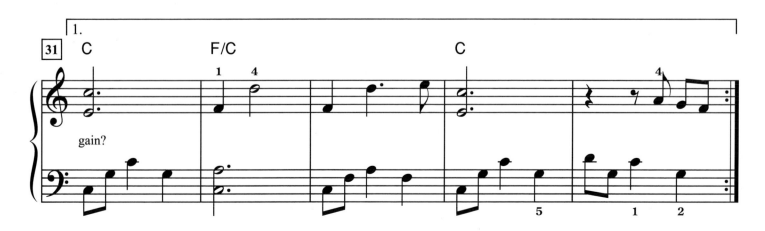

1.

31 C   F/C   C

gain?

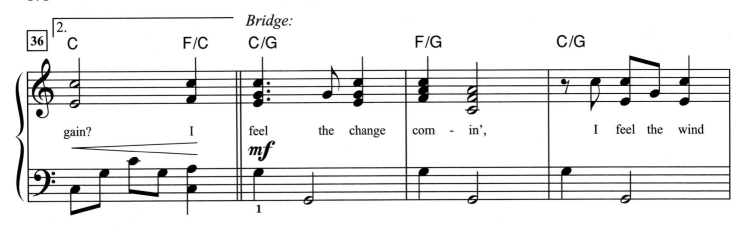

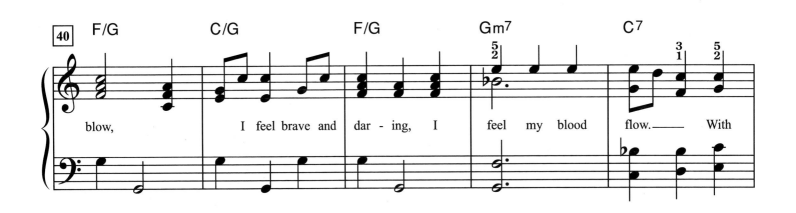

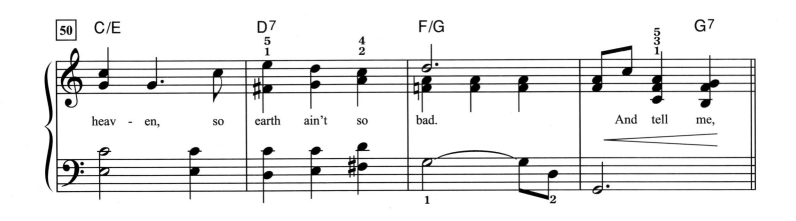

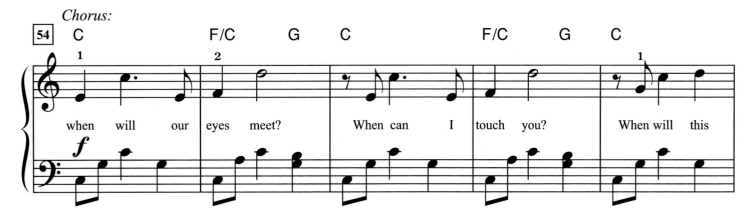

Chorus:

when will our eyes meet? When can I touch you? When will this

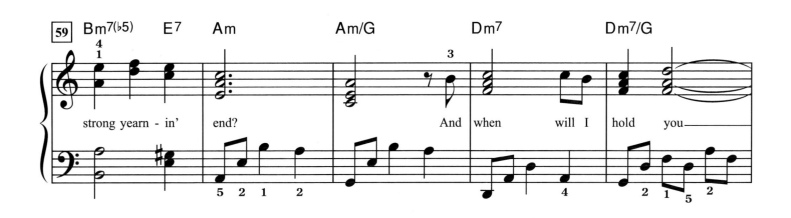

strong yearn - in' end? And when will I hold you

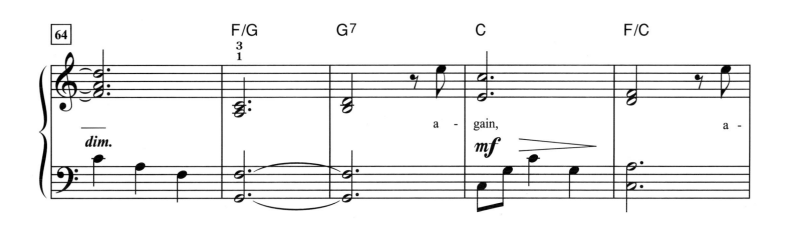

dim. a - gain, *mf* a -

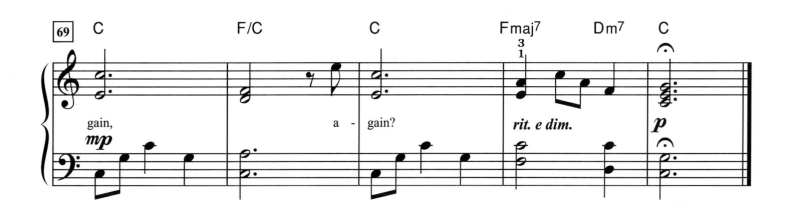

gain, *mp* a - gain? *rit. e dim.* *p*

THE WIND BENEATH MY WINGS

Words and Music by
Larry Henley and Jeff Silbar
Arranged by Dan Coates

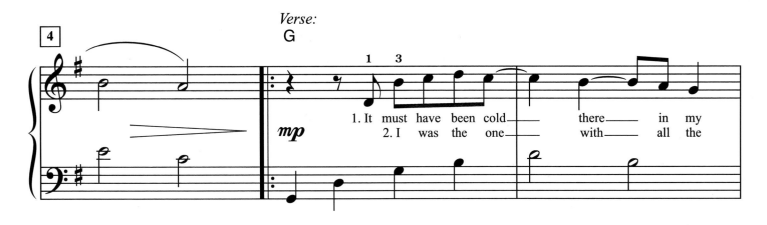

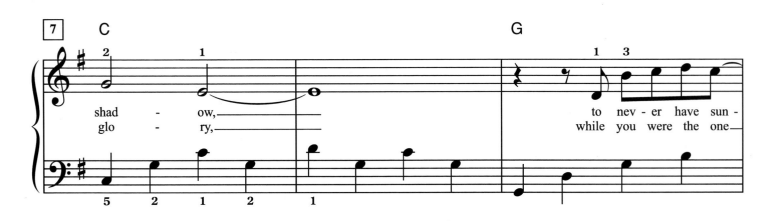

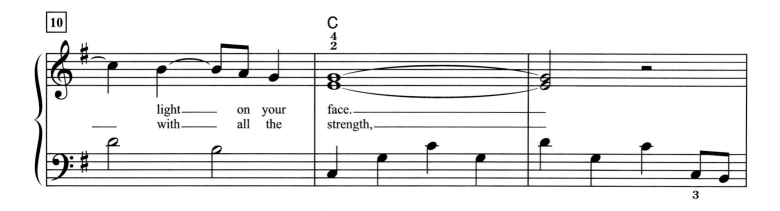

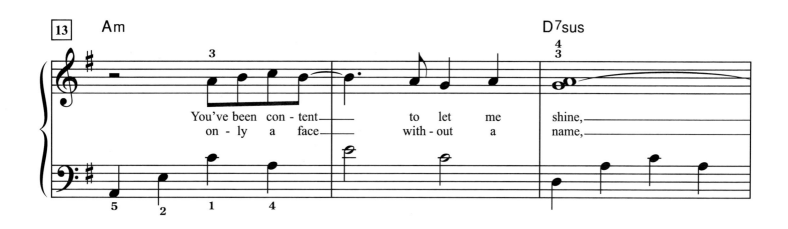

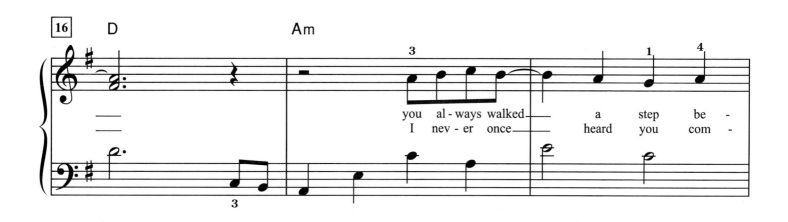

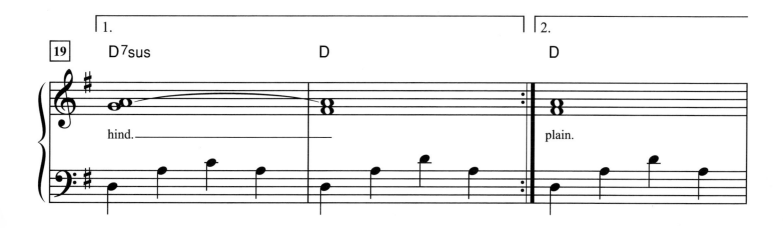

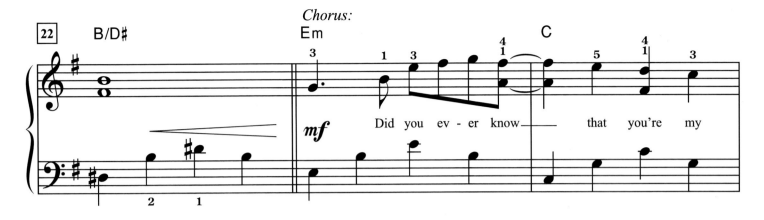

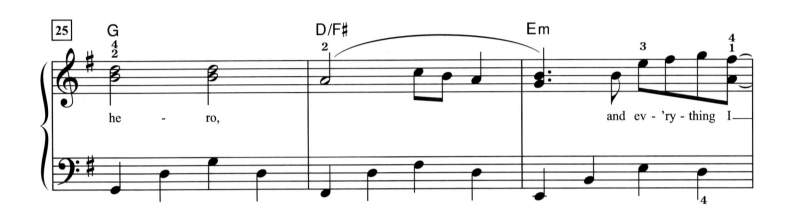

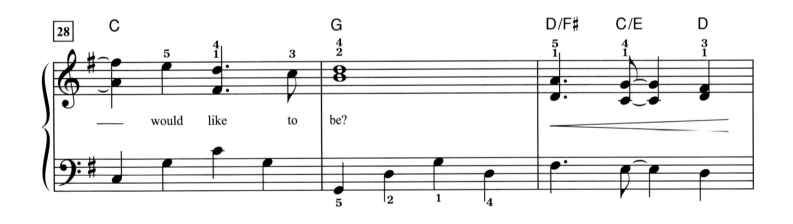

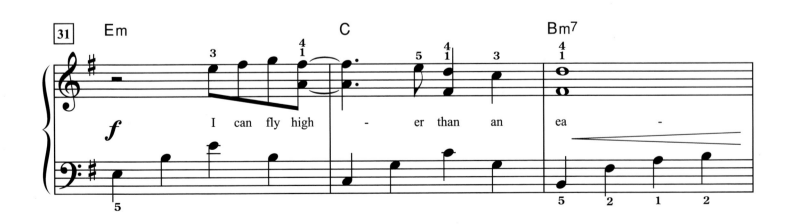

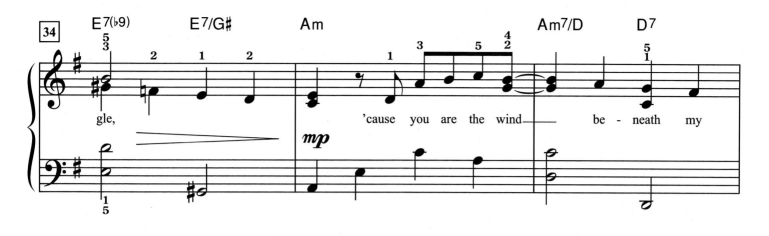

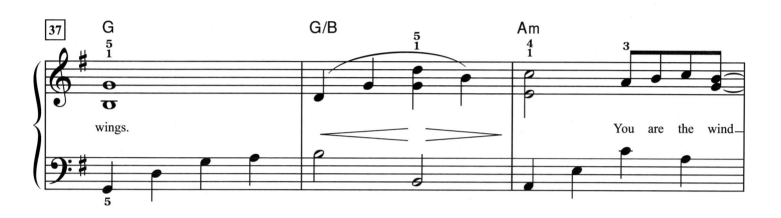

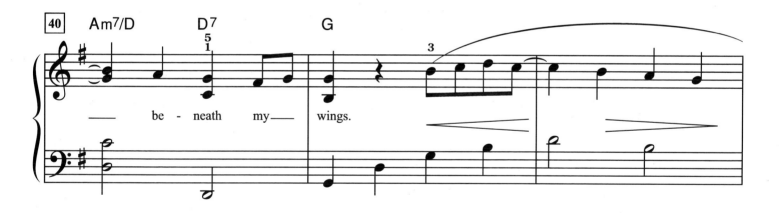

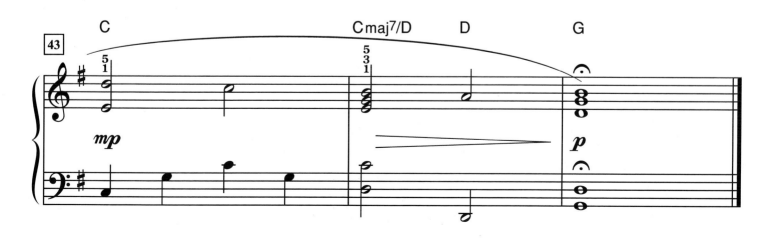

YOU HAVEN'T SEEN THE LAST OF ME

(from *Burlesque*)

Words and Music by Diane Warren
Arranged by Dan Coates

Slowly

Verse:

1. Feel - ing bro - ken, bare - ly hold - ing on,
2. *See additional lyrics.*

but there's still some - thing so strong some - where in - side me.

And I am down, but I'll be up a - gain. Don't count me out just yet.

Chorus:

I've been brought down to my

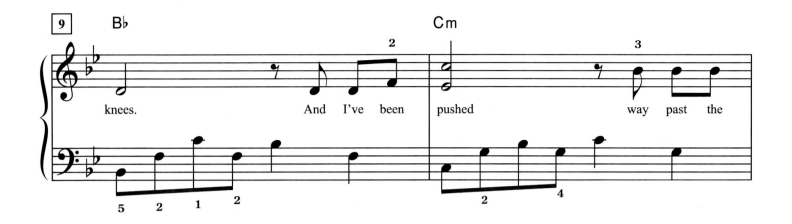

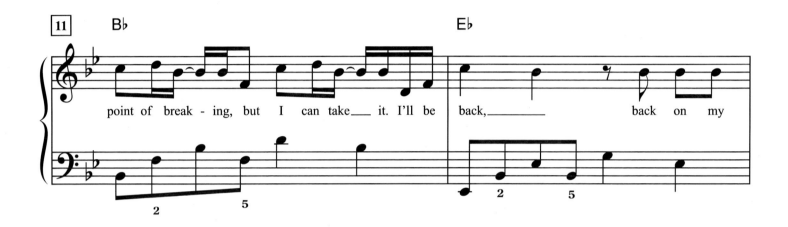

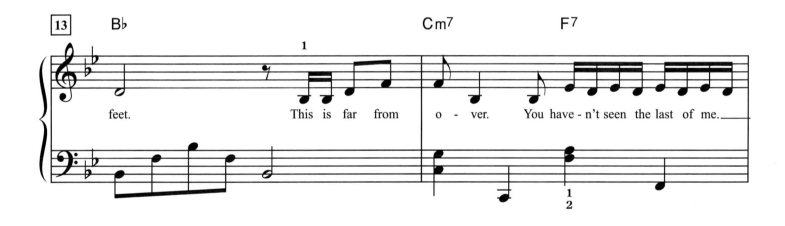

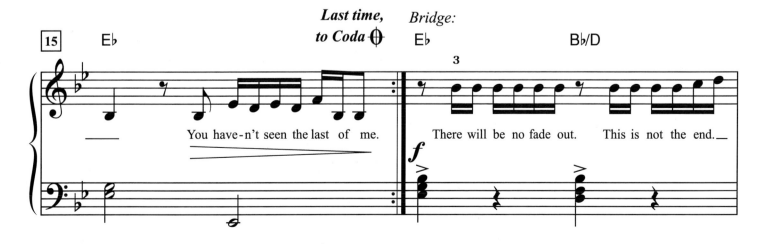

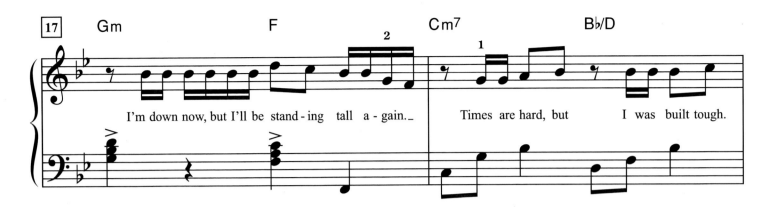

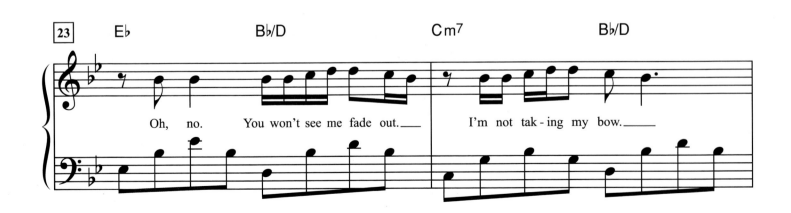

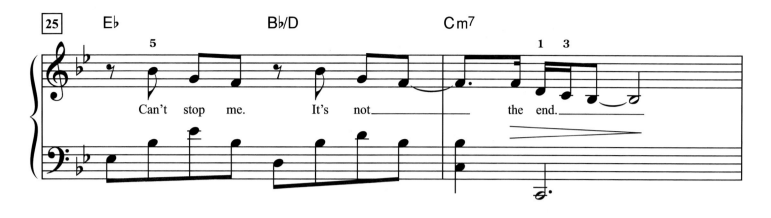

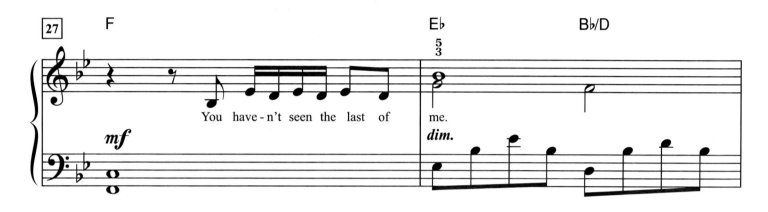

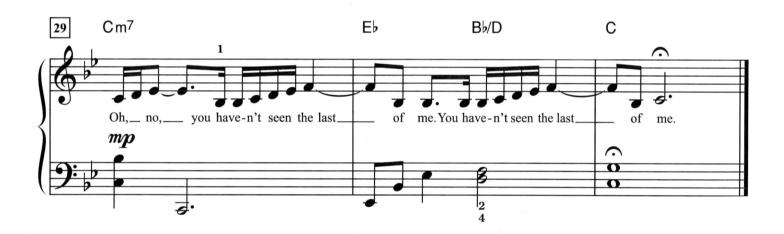

Verse 2:
They can say that I won't stay around,
But I'm gonna stand my ground.
You're not gonna stop me.
You don't know me, you don't know who I am.
Don't count me out so fast.
(To Chorus:)

YOU LIGHT UP MY LIFE

Words and Music by Joe Brooks
Arranged by Dan Coates

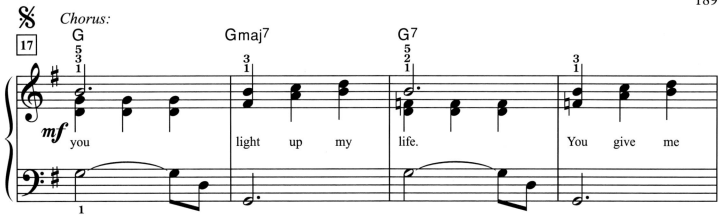

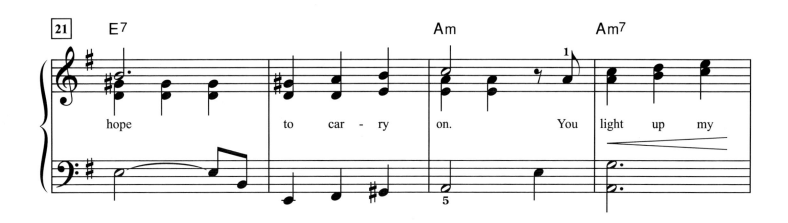

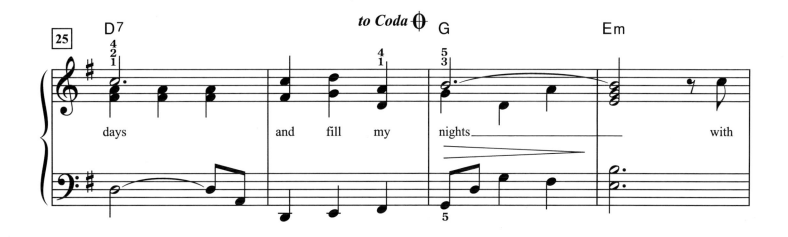

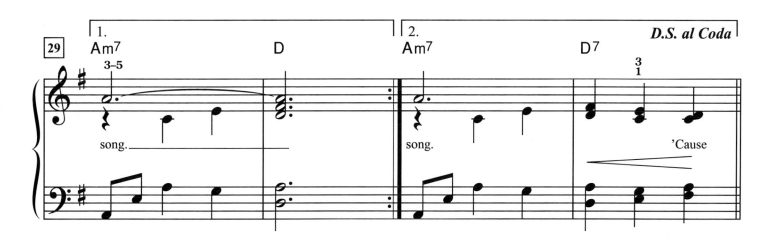

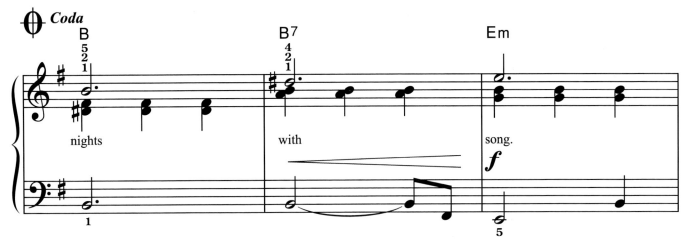

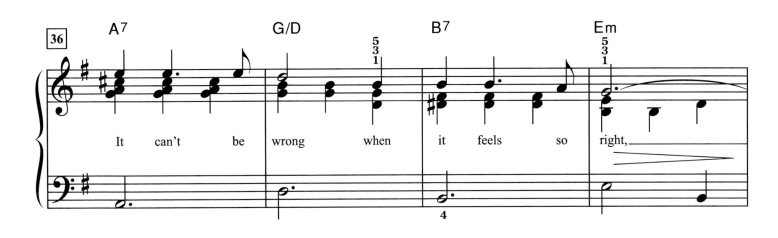

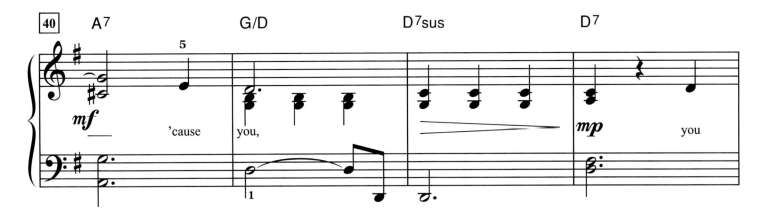

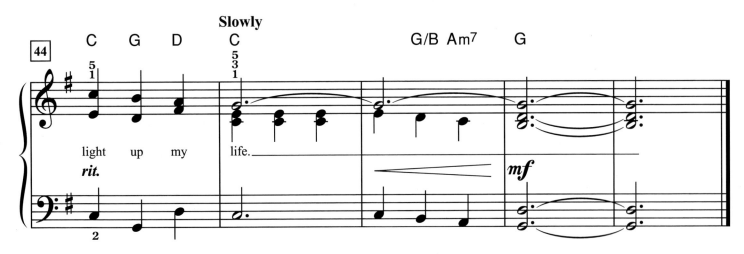

YOU RAISE ME UP

Words and Music by
Rolf Lovland and Brendan Graham
Arranged by Dan Coates

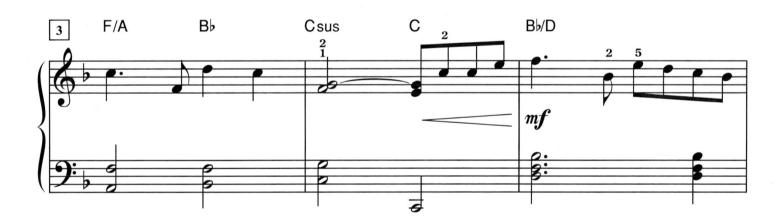

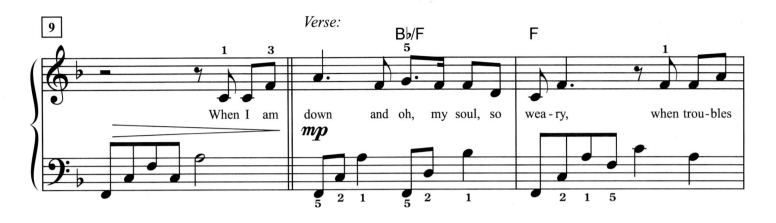

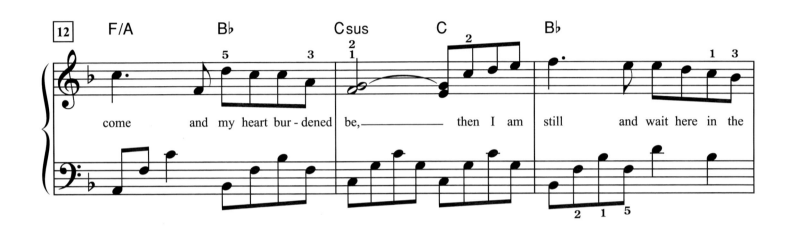

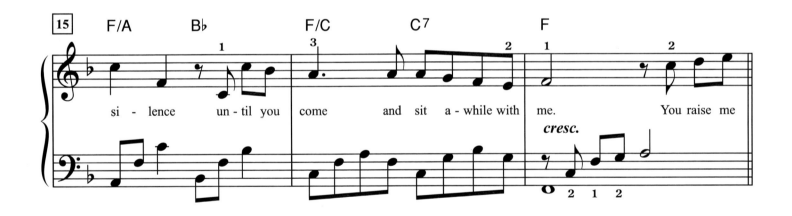

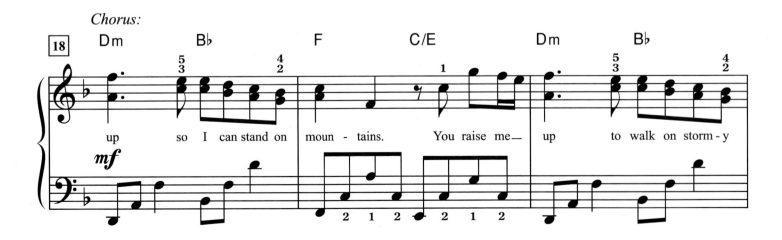

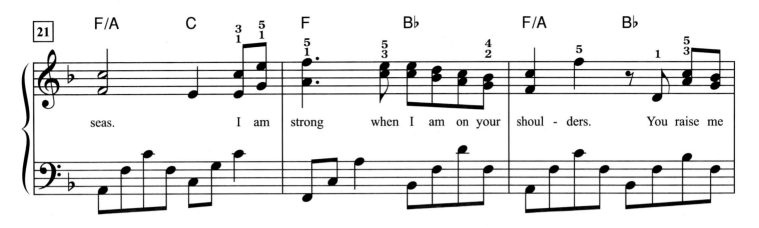

seas.   I am strong   when I am on your   shoul - ders.   You raise me

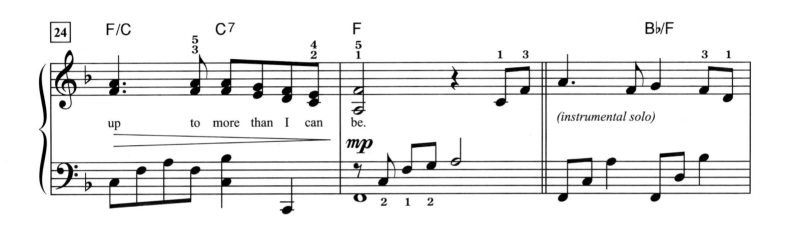

up   to more than I can   be.   *(instrumental solo)*

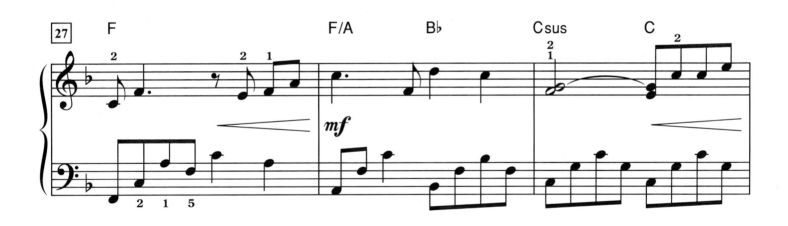

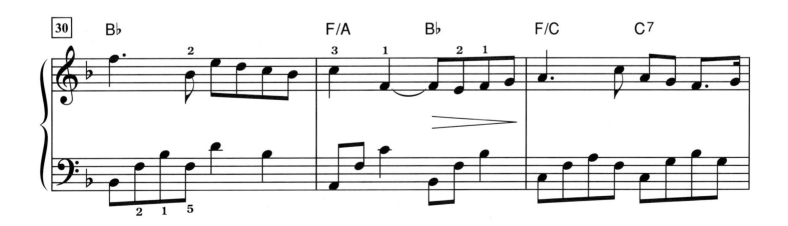

Chorus:

You raise me up so I can stand on moun - tains. You raise me —

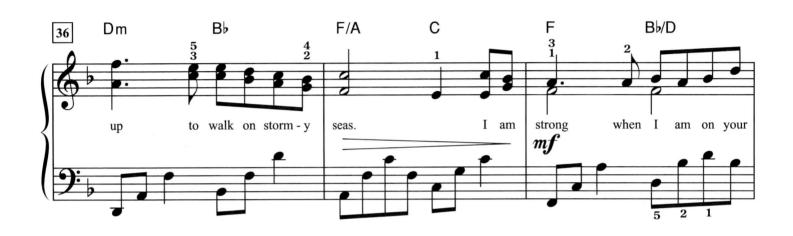

up to walk on storm - y seas. I am strong when I am on your

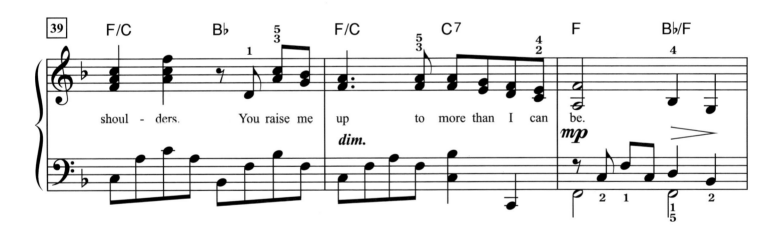

shoul - ders. You raise me up to more than I can be.

Chorus:

You raise me up so I can stand on moun - tains. You raise me —